When You're Ready For The Fairytale

What To Do While Waiting For The Prince

Volume 1

"Getting Ready"

Daphne M. Hunter

When You're Ready For The Fairytale

What To Do While Waiting For The Prince

Volume 1: "Getting Ready"

By

Daphne M. Hunter

Published By:

ABM Publications
A division of Andrew Bills Ministries Inc.
PO Box 6811, Orange, CA 92863

ISBN: 978-1-931820-76-9

DEDICATION

The Most Romantic Person I know

My Father God

As it was He who wrote my Godly Fairytale Romance

The Romance that far surpassed my dreams

My Sisters who love and trusted me enough

To venture out in search of their own

Godly Fairytale Romances

As I led the way based on the promises of

Our Daddy God

My Spiritual Mama

For Loving Me, Accepting Me, Believing In Me & With Me

For The Mighty Man of God & the Birth of a God Dream

And especially for Our Friday Mornings In the Word & In
Prayer

My Brother, My Friend & the Mighty Man of God

The Decoy

Who God used to prepare me for

The Man of God of my Life

To My Children,

Kiana, Jordan & Benjamin

For Recognizing and Calling Me Cinderella

For Your Faith, Prayers and Belief in the Journey

And in The Mighty Man of God whom is to Enter Our Lives

May He Be the Spiritual Leader That We Can Only Dream
Of

AND...

To My Hero, Husband & Mighty Man of God of My Life

The only person I would want to do life with

Whomever You May Be

TABLE OF CONTENTS

An Invitation from The Author

You are invited to an intense Bible study whether individually or with a group of God's Girls, who believe God for their marriages and for future husbands, The Mighty Men of God!

God's Girls are family and we need each other! We need to be able to feel safe, to be able to share, to cover each other in prayer, stay in agreement and come along side during the bumpy ride of change and transformation as each of us sisters are about to embark on an adventure to see what God has in store for us!

We are all different and so will our relationships with the Lord and our pace in the race we're in towards discovering our Men of God. Some of you are still stretching and warming up, which means you have just come to the positive realization you desire a Godly Husband, also known as a Man of God and now ready to make the first step towards that goal. Some of you are in the starting blocks; meaning I know I want a Man of God in my life but don't know what to do towards believing God for it, just give you a "starting line and you're off". Some of you have started the race and realize you need a carrot in front of you to keep you going. Meaning you still believe for the Man of God and have been for a long time but growing weary in waiting. Then there are others that are sprinting, you see the finish line in sight and the Man of God will be here before you know it!

Regardless, where we are at, we need each other and we need accountability! That's why I strongly urge you to meet in a group. God has great things ahead for all of us and He wants His Princesses to have their Fairytales!

I thank you for allowing me the privilege to share my heart with you and to be a part of your incredibly personal journey with you. I want to encourage each of you until you get closer to becoming the desired Bride for Christ and for His representation of your husband on earth!

Remember God has not forgotten you! God truly wants to do something about the desire you carry in your heart for your Mighty Man of God!

So, get ready for the ride of your life with your God, the King!

A Single Woman's Prayer

As a single woman ...I seek You, God to guide me and direct every step I take. I won't look at others to complete me because I have you as my companion, lover, friend, brother, father, and Lord. Help me to be complete in You, Lord. You created me with a purpose and I know your desire is for me to wait for your best. I do hereby commit myself to you, to remain pure and set apart until I marry. I ask You Father, to prepare the man you created to be my husband as you prepare me to be the wife he desires. In time, we will meet face-to-face and he will receive me as you have received me. I pray that we will have a heart after You, Father, and that the joy of the Lord will be our strength in our love for you, each other and for the mission you call us to do together.

In Jesus name

Amen.

DAPHNE M. HUNTER

**Every man's life is a fairy tale,
written by God's fingers**

-   Hans Christian Andersen

DAPHNE M. HUNTER

Preface

The title reads, When You're Ready For The Fairytale, but what is the fairytale? The fairytale is the promised, blessed abundant life God wants His children to have. The fairytale doesn't just happen magically; one must be ready to experience it. To be ready for the fairytale, you must be willing to do the work to have it. Work is always involved when there's anything worth having. This book is based on private, intimate conversations I have had with God, plus what I have learned in preparing for my own fairytale. The only reason you now hold my heart on these pages is because God has given me a heart with so much passion for others.

I have a passion to see others obtain their God-Dreams. A God-Dream is not a dream you conjure up, but the dream God desires for you to have. It's your life's purpose; calling and you will find no deeper satisfaction until you're working towards it. This God-Dream can take form as a desire to own a business, to have a specific career, help your community, to have a family, be involved in ministry service, to improve yourself and your relationships, etc. or all the above. This book specifically targets working on improving yourself, while waiting and believing God for the God-Dream. Let's face it regardless of what your God-Dream is, YOU are the common denominator of whatever it is you want and God cannot trust you with the God-Dream until you're ready for it.

For you to be ready for the Fairytale, which is the accomplishment of the God-Dream in every area of your life, you need to seek the most important relationship of your life. That's a relationship with God, by doing so you will begin to find, understand and improve on the real you. Then you'll be ready to experience better relationships, because nobody is meant to do life alone. When you can offer the best YOU there is, then God will bring amazing people into your life and ultimately, the love match of your life. This book is simply about not settling for anything less than God's best for your life.

So you will find this book discusses the area of preparing for the most intimate of human relationships, marriage. If your Fairytale includes the God-Dream of wanting to be married, you must realize that No God-Dream will materialize without intimacy. Intimacy requires honesty. You must learn to be honest with God, yourself and then with others. Only then will you be ready for a husband. If you are already married, then you are set with the right love match for you and are welcome to read the book as a reminder to be the best YOU, for God, yourself and your husband.

As you know, our world has fallen from what our God and Creator had intended from the beginning. The moment Adam and Eve sinned, they hid from God out of their fear, shame and dishonesty. Therefore, they hid their hearts as well as their bodies from Him. As a result, we innately do the same. Our lives and cultures reflect that fact. So this is a book for the women, who are ready to get it right. If that is you, then I call you a princess or soon to become one, regardless of what marital status label you have been given.

This book is for the princesses, the Daughters of God. The single princesses, whether never been married, divorced or widowed who choose to believe God to give them their future husband. This includes those women that have experienced broken promises, broken hearts and as well as contributing to doing some of the breaking of promises and hearts of others whether before or after asking Jesus into their life. God has forgiven you of that. Also for the married princesses, that are so busy, distracted or depleted and forget how to be all that you're created to be for God, yourself and for your husband. ALL God's Daughters deserve a second chance to get life right and in order, regardless of background, age, race, marital status, etc., for God is a second chance God.

I am not an authority on relationships, even in the area I am sharing. This book is not a "how to get a man" guide nor must you follow it exactly as depicted, everyone is unique, so I trust you will "tweak" the instructions and/or homework to custom fit your life. This book is simply a guideline of what I have done and am still doing in working on my testimony as I continue to believe God for all He has for me. God told me to write this book for all of those who would dare pick it up and believe for themselves. This book is a message of hard work, faith, hope and love. The love we yearn for from our Heavenly Father, our Lord and Savior, and True Husband, Jesus Christ and of our Godly earthly husband-to-be.

Scripture says, "It is impossible to please God without faith." (Hebrews 11:6) Do you have faith? What is faith? Faith is something (or someone) hoped for but the evidence of it (or him) not being seen (Hebrews 11:1). To have this faith in believing and hoping for a Godly husband and do nothing about it would be in vain. (James 2:17) Instead of taking matters into your own hands, we will be putting them in God's.

So this book will assist you to stretch your faith. It is this very faith, that will be exercised to give you hope along the journey as you will be led to the love of your life (as long as you allow God to remain in control). I will join my faith with yours to first of all, to experience love in your relationship with God and then with the love He sends you to be your companion for life. As Jesus is our true Hope of Glory (Colossians 1:27), we also want our romantic relationship to glorify Him and then we will have an all-encompassing love. With God involved in our fairytale romance and marriage, this will prove that a threefold cord is not easily broken (Ecclesiastes 4:12).

You will be reading my heart on these pages as God has told me to share with you my own in-progress testimony, the private and very personal conversations we have had together. How could I share such secrets? It is simple. I love God more than anything, including more so than my own personal comfort. My obedience is proof of my love and I cannot deny Him. I did it for that reason; although, knowing my obedience will bring me a blessing; however, He chooses to deliver it. I already know that by writing this book, I have overcome my fear of writing, the fear of walking this journey alone and the fear of commitment. Therefore, I made the decision that no one else would have to walk their singleness journey alone as long as they would take me along with them while they read my heart on these pages. My experiences are offered to validate their own experiences, fears, and heartaches. As you will soon discover, I purposely didn't write this book to simply be read, but wrote it so the reader, my friend, would feel as if we were talking across the table face-to-face and heart-to-heart. I'm being real honest and vulnerable in order to encourage you to be the same with yourself. Only then will real progress be made and you'll be well on your way to beginning your fairytale. Remember true fairytales are not sweet and glorious, but full of obstacles, heartaches, challenges and fears to overcome regardless of whatever twists and turns the adventure brings. So I may or may not discuss the details of what I physically experienced I will give you lots of food for thought from all my mental, social and spiritual experiences that have caused me to grow, mature and help me to be ready to be someone's Bride-to-be.

It all started with a request. God asked me to go on this journey to trust Him to lead me to a special someone He has chosen just for me. Then He asked would I reveal my heart to encourage you to allow Him to do the same. I cannot emphasize the importance I sensed of His desire of wanting you to dare accept this quest. I knew that whatever He would ask of me was my reasonable service to Him. I'll never forget when God said to me, "Daphne, there's a time when your testimony is no longer yours, but mine." I knew instantly what He meant, that I am to share my testimony with whomever He brings before me and when He tells me. These writings recount conversations I have had with Him and others. I have witnessed wondrous and miraculous relationships form as a result based on His words of encouragement and homework. There's Homework? Yes! Like I told you, anything worth having does require some work; don't worry, it will be worthwhile work. You will need a Holy Bible (any translation), pen and a homework journal. All homework assignments are listed at the end of each chapter. So, let's get started.

Chapter 1

Born a Princess

Have you ever noticed girls have this innate dream to be a princess? We believe a princess' life is so much more magical, exciting, and better than the kind of life we are presently living. There is some truth to this, but before I can reveal the truth I must uncover the lie.

What we don't know is, we are already princesses. No wonder we desire such a thing, a title, a position because it was already ours to begin with. The lie is the deception that we are not princesses. So we dream of obtaining something we already have. We wish and hope for this and suffer from all the "if only" thoughts when we were already born into it. You don't have to try to become what you already are; you simply accept who and what you are and "walk-in" to your role, title, position and ultimately your authority. Simply embrace it.

You won't see yourself as a princess until you realize and know without a doubt who your Father is. Obviously, to be a princess, that means your Daddy is the King, meaning God. You're not a princess because you deserve it. You're a princess because of who your Daddy is.

The bigger your Daddy is in your eyes, the more worthy you become to yourself. This gives new meaning to "how big is your Daddy?" How big is your God? When Satan, the enemy, attacks you with doubt and unbelief, just like a little girl would, you tell him your Daddy can beat him up...and DID!

However, without a relationship with God, you will always be a little girl struggling to find yourself and never accomplishing all your Daddy has planned for your life. This is the lifelong strategy of the enemy to deceive you into believing you're nothing special, that you have nothing to offer, that you will never succeed or ever obtain the promise. If you believe his lie then you can't put up a fight. You will stay weak, broken and bound, with his foot on your neck rather than yours on his.

To break out of this mentality you have to make a conscious decision to not take it anymore. Say to yourself, "I am a princess.

Being a princess isn't about me, but it's up to me. It was by my Daddy's design, I didn't ask for it so I can't help it. I just accept it and represent Him well. He loved me so much He calls me His princess and I am Daddy's little girl." Receiving Him and His love is the first step of accepting your title of being a princess and stepping into your role. Are you still doubtful about being a princess?

See for yourself in the Bible, which is the infallible, God-breathed Word of God, the Truth. The evidence of who you are can be found in these scriptures. You need a personal relationship with the King and then you will have the full right to become the princess you have always dreamt of being. If you don't have a personal relationship with God, you need to do this. Please go to the back of the book to the Do You Want to Become a Princess? page then read and repeat the prayer. Then come back and read on and see who you were created to be.

Read the following scriptures:

John 1:12-13

Romans 8:14-17

Jeremiah 1:5

2 Corinthians 6:18

Galatians 4:6

1 John 3:1

Romans 8:37

See? You are a princess! Even if you don't feel like it, you simply begin to believe it! Have you ever made decisions you wish you hadn't made? Take a moment, do you recall ever thinking, I know there is a bigger plan for my life than this? Why am I settling for this when I know I can do so much better? This is proof that the princess in you is being oppressed, begging to come out, to be whom and what she is created and called to be. So let her! You'll be glad you did. Then your life will actually become easier to live and it will become easier to make the right decisions. Why? Listening to your heart gets easier because you allowed Daddy into your life and heart. It's now easier for Him to reveal His desires for your life and for you to obey what He asks of you.

Being a princess comes with a lot of "perks". That's why little girls believe that being a princess is so much fun and exciting.

You don't have to tell a little girl that being a princess is exciting; she just knows, so it must be true. The biggest "perk" to being a princess is being well matched to a prince. This is why we girls enjoy fairytales. We have several fairytales to choose from such as; Cinderella, Sleeping Beauty, and Snow White. All of them are princesses; they all look different, have different characteristics, talents, responsibilities and each one has her own prince. Little girls lavish all their love on their Daddy and then venture out wanting to love a prince of their own. It's natural to want this, because if Daddy created us to be princesses then He created princes for us to marry.

What if the wrong prince married the wrong princess in these stories? It wouldn't have a "happily ever after" ending. We see this so often in the world today and they endure unnecessary obstacles, only if they had waited and trusted their Daddy, the King. Even when the right prince and princess are betrothed, still their life has twists, turns and struggles, and they're supposed to, but the obstacles are more easily conquered by those joined together by God. No couple experiences a perfect, stress and problem free life. How much fun would life be together if everything was perfect?

Without obstacles, what would the prince be fighting for other than to provide for and protect his princess? It's his princess who gives him honor and courage to go out and do battle yet again day after day. When the prince and princess realize that the goal in their modern day life is to take on each obstacle as an opportunity to overcome and they have a dragon to slay together. How do they do this? They must support each other only then will they be victorious. If the prince and princess are at odds with each other the division between them gives the dragon/enemy the upper hand and can destroy them both. Their everyday small or large victories are their "happily ever after" until the next obstacle comes.

So, dear princess, are you ready to meet your prince? Your Daddy only wants you happy and fulfilled in this area of your life, as you will be in every area of your life as long as you allow Daddy to rule. The moment you make the decision to read further and do what lies before you in these pages it will bring you closer to your prince. How can I say that? I believe. I love our Daddy so much and felt His heavy heart for you. I asked Him, "Daddy, what is it? What can I do for you?" He said, "Show and tell my beautiful daughters, my princesses, the plans I have for them, the Godly fairytale romances I have awaiting them IF they will allow me to write them." Here I am because of Him, because of you and because I stepped out and dared to take our Daddy at His word of having a Godly fairytale romance. In fact, I've heard others share their Godly inspired love stories and deeply desire for you to experience yours. So, take your time and go through this book at your own pace. If you are ready, let's get started, Beautiful Princess.

Again I ask you...if you don't have a personal relationship with your Daddy (God), please stop reading any further. Please go to the back of the book to the Do You Want to Become a Princess? page then read the prayer out loud, and contact me to tell me that you have taken the first step towards beginning the most incredible journey of your life! I invite you to start being the princess that you are today!

DAPHNE M. HUNTER

Chapter 2

Where Do I Begin?

You may simply not know how and where to start. I understand having the desire to move forward in life, wanting to improve your relationships and more specifically with your relationship with God. Learning to truly trust God with your love life isn't easy. Those are legitimate feelings. Giving yourself time is moving forward.

I felt the same way and I am simply sharing what I did. I am not saying that you need to follow every suggestion exactly the way I did. Simply receive what I have suggested, take it to God in prayer then "tweak" the suggestions based on your personality and relationship with God. Allow God to lead you in this very delicate, intimate and special area of your life. No one knows you better than He does. You are in the best and most capable hands of all, His.

Everything begins with God. Your first commitment should be to Him. Only then will you have established a solid foundation before embarking on this journey. Your commitment to your relationship with God will teach you and reveal to you how truly ready you are for the God ordained mate He has predestined for you. Why do I say that? Without a solid commitment to God, you give yourself the opportunity to back out or quit trusting God to bring His choice of a Godly Man into your life. To those of you who have not considered a relationship with a strong Godly Christian man; this is the only way to go. These men are the princes; they have the same Daddy God as you. Also, do not use God, in hopes of finally having that husband. Daddy knows your heart and your motives; selfish motives and wrong attitudes may only delay the process even longer. Be sincere with God, your foundational relationship with Him means everything.

You will discover that you need healing, there is a lot going on inside of you. Usually when we want something else or someone else, or even want something or someone to change, keep in mind that means we are not going to escape having to make some changes ourselves. In order to be prepared to welcome our prince we need to be honest with God and ourselves. We've all been through a lot in our lives and it would be ridiculous to think those experiences haven't impacted us. So we need to come face to face with some of those things we have suppressed or are holding onto whether we are aware that we are doing it or not. Basically, we need to grow into the stately princesses that we are. We need to mature in new areas, into new levels with God, with ourselves and as a Godly wife in training. This preparation will aid you into becoming the future wife and mother your husband and children will need. This healing process is all encompassing. All that is left to ask is, "Are you ready to commit, to surrender the most personal part of your life to God? Do you trust Him to choose your lifelong partner and bring the prince to you and present you the, princess, to him? Are you willing to be completely honest with God and yourself? Are you willing not to run from this like you may have from other things? Quitting is not an option after making this commitment; otherwise, what is the point? How badly do you want your fairytale? The fairytale isn't just about the Man of God (future husband/aka MOG) in your life, it is just the beginning. However, it could be the bait to get your attention to move you both into the plan God has for your lives. Isn't there always more?"

Take a moment to think over if you are truly serious about committing your "love life" to God. Are you willing to follow His ways and not your own? Are you ready to make this commitment to yourself? When you honestly believe you are ready then you are welcome to enter the "Commitment Ceremony" between you and God.

Before continuing, I strongly recommend that if you do not have a personal relationship with Jesus that should absolutely be the first step. Notice this is my third time asking you? It's that important. If this is your heart's desire, please go to the back of the book to the Do You Want to Become a Princess? page then read the prayer out loud and contact me so I know you have become a born again princess! Without Jesus as Lord and Savior of your life, your commitment will not be solid to Him, to yourself or even to your future husband. Should you already have the most important relationship already in place please continue reading.

Congratulations on your decision! Now, allow me to explain about the purpose of a Promise Ring (or Purity Ring) in your Commitment Ceremony. This promise ring is your engagement ring from Jesus to you and will be used in the Commitment Ceremony. Jesus needs to be your focus, as He will prepare you for the journey you're about to take. He will see you through to completion. (Philippians 1:6) He will never leave you or ignore you

(Hebrews 13:5). Being alone may be an improvement compared to the relationships you have experienced in the past. After your prince is in your life, Jesus doesn't leave. Jesus sees your relationship through until you're married. You will want Him to be involved in your marriage after He has already proven Himself faithful from the day you make this commitment to your wedding day and for eternity.

Everything that happens in the natural is first created in the spiritual realm. It is our faith believing in the unseen that makes it appear before our very eyes and becomes real to us. So, by making this commitment and entering into the "Commitment Ceremony" you are experiencing your "Spiritual Wedding Day" today while believing for the manifestation of your Wedding Day in the natural later. Now you are ready to enter into the "Commitment Ceremony". During this ceremony you are to commit yourself to waiting on the Lord to bring your Mighty Man of God, if you're single or to strengthen your husband's relationship with God if you're married.

Please read on and follow the instructions carefully to conduct the Commitment Ceremony with your own Promise Ring.

God often has me minister to Singles about remaining pure by being celibate and combat loneliness with journal writing, while waiting on Him to send His appointed mate for them. This really works! God also gave me other significant instructions to keep me busy and focused; such as, developing my relationship with Him while learning how to be the wife my Man of God will need me to be. After heeding His instructions, I learned to meditate on His promises within His Word. Then He led me to His ultimate promise, His very first relational creation, the God instituted relationship called marriage. Marriage is a promise not only to our spouse but to Him, too.

You fulfill many roles in your life such as being a daughter, friend, student, co-worker, etc. in your everyday life. You will do the same in the Kingdom of God. First, once you have entered into a relationship with God, you become the Daughter of the Most High God, the King, making you a princess. Then you are betrothed to the King's Son, Jesus, making Him your first love. Later you will be given to a prince, the Man of God, which is a Christian man that has a sincere, intimate relationship with God as you do. Make sure your Man of God, the prince, loves the Lord Jesus more than you, only then can he love you the way you deserve and then some. Then there won't be anything he won't do for you. He will model this from Jesus, as it says in Ephesians 5:25. Jesus promised He would return for us, His bride. As we make ourselves ready as the Bride of Christ, this aids us in preparing to be a bride for the Man of God. Once our preparation is complete, we are then no longer princesses, but become queens. Get ready to learn, grow, heal and receive the royal treatment you have longed for and deserve!

Like any promise, it needs to be solidified. In order to do this, something of value must be established. For example, a promise to marry, is like a contract, Biblically it's called, an agreement of Covenant. We, women know a man's intention and promise is proven tangibly by presenting a ring. That's why we ladies expect an engagement ring when the man proposes. Jesus proved His love and commitment to you, not by offering a ring, but by sacrificing His life. No one has ever loved you that much. Keep that in mind as it's so easy to get lost in dreaming of the mate to come in the natural. I want you to look to Jesus as your Bridegroom. Matthew 6:33 promises that if you make Jesus first, your top priority then all the rest will be given to you. So, get your mind off of a physical mate! Who better to focus on than the Supernatural one we already have! Who has proven Himself faithful in every area of our lives, more so than we can imagine. So, why don't we trust Him more? Why do we focus more on a man than Jesus? Because our flesh is weak and we allow our flesh-led thoughts and emotions rule us. When we permit our minds to wander, or when we choose to whine (which is nothing more than cursing not blessing) rather than wait (be patient), we begin to destroy the work God is doing within your relationship with Him and in the one He is trying to build with His appointed mate for you. What can you do to prevent destroying what He is building? Simply believe (have faith) in Him that He is working everything out for you. Remind yourself of that when your flesh-led emotions want to control you (instead of your Spirit).

In hopes to offer you a positive reinforcement to prevent you from fleeing from God's promise, forgetting His love and passion for you, please let this Promise Ring be a tangible reminder that His promises are real and on their way to you if you're willing to hold on and press on. When you feel ready to call it quits look at your Promise Ring and ask yourself these questions. "Do I really want to choose a mate for myself? Do I think I can do a better job than God? Wasn't it me that decided to enter this commitment? Didn't I decide to purchase this book? God's Promise Ring is a symbol to me and to Him that I am willing to wait and let Him be in control of my romantic life. Especially, because I saw the damage I can do by choosing a mate for myself. How about this question...If I trust God with my spirit, soul, life, body, finances why can't I trust Him with my heart and His timing?"

When you answer these questions and you don't know what to say or if you do, but don't like the answers, rededicate yourself to your Promise to God and to yourself. Isn't that what a marriage is all about? If you cheat on your promise with God, won't you cheat on your mate? And if you would cheat on your mate then are you really ready for God to send you His appointed spouse just for you? Remember the heart of your Godly Spouse is just as important, as precious and as tender as yours. God won't allow you to break their heart anymore than He will allow them to break yours. Now, isn't God truly good? Gives you a new meaning to He knows us better than we know ourselves, doesn't it? With all this in mind, how can we not trust Him, or the future spouse He's selected for us and within His timing. God Bless You in your personal journey as you allow God to be God and write the wondrous most amazing Love Story of all time...YOURS!

Please know that I am agreeing with you now, even at this present moment that I type this prayer as well as time and time again for the one who holds and reads these heartfelt words on paper later. There is power in agreement as the Word of God says, "Again I say to you that if two of you agree on earth concerning anything that they ask, it will be done for them by My Father in heaven." (Matthew 18:19 NKJV)

(NOTE: Married Princesses: Use this same prayer to commit your husband to the Lord recognizing he only comes second to God. Ask God to bless, renew, rejuvenate and restore your marriage for His purpose and glory.)

Now pray these words and know my heart is with you and feel free to write, create and say our own personal vows to God. Go ahead, marry Him!

Lord, your word tells us that there is such power in agreement and I know your word will not return void. It must do what it has been sent out to do, so I confidently pray in agreement with my sister for the husband of your choosing not mine/hers . Your word tells us that you knew us before the foundation of the world, while we were within our mother's womb, and that you have a plan, a hope and a future for us. Our future includes a Man of God, a husband by our side because you gave us the desire to be married. We are calling and speaking them into existence into our lives today. We know we cannot please you without faith so we have combined our faith and putting that faith into action by entering into a Covenant with you this day. We are unable to enter into a Marriage Covenant with our natural spouse at this time, but we have nothing stopping us from entering into one with Our One and Only reigning Bridegroom that has already betrothed Himself to us in which He paid the ultimate price with His Blood. With this Promise Ring I will engage myself into the Will and Plan of God for my life to wait on the Lord for my Wedding Day here and the one to come.

On this day (enter the date) _____,
I vow to you, my personal Lord and Savior that I will honor my vow of celibacy. I surrender to you and permit you to deal with me and to heal me. So that I may be more ready than I think I am, so that I can be 100% without a doubt ready to honor and cherish the gift you will give me in the spouse you are in the process of sending me. Thank you, Jesus for your faithfulness, for completing what you have

started. I thank you now for all you've done and all you're yet to do for me in my vapor time here called life. Let my life bring you more glory by accepting you to fulfill me in this way. Let my decision be a Holy and acceptable offering to you, to please you, in your precious and mighty name, Jesus, I pray. Amen.

I may not have been with you physically to pray with you, but trust me I was with you in spirit. Thank you for allowing me to be a part of a truly tender moment in your life. If you don't think so, it is and it's your Spiritual Wedding Day. When you became saved you felt Jesus tug at your heart and you knew you needed a Savior, a relationship with Him. You found Him that day and now know that He is and can be your everything. What makes today different is today He revealed Himself to you in a different way. In a way you didn't realize until you made a decision to allow Him. Today He became the "Lover of Your Soul", your Bridegroom and you, His Bride.

Now from me to you...These words, this book and this ring all came from God, He simply placed it on my heart to write just like it says in Habakkuk 2:2-3. I was told to share with those that are lonely, despaired and yearning for the Godly mate they're praying for, whether single or married. Here is His answer for you until the time comes. I know this and His journal teaching that He has given me to share will bless you to endure. As for me as a vessel, I request one thing of you if I could and if you are willing. Please write or email me of God's faithfulness to you by sharing your testimony of how this book aided you in your time of need or to share your beautiful and incredible love story with me about that Godly Husband we prayed for. God bless you. His Servant, ~Daphne

Now that you have completed the "Commitment Ceremony", here is what you must do next. I am going to give you some homework. You didn't know that this was an interactive book did you? Well, it is and it's good for you. You are going to begin an adventure on another set of pages, in a book called Your MOG/Husband Journal. This journal is your intimate companion for now. It is between you, God and the Mighty Man of God that will enter your life at God's appointed time.

For you wives, this journal is for you to share of your journey to becoming a "new" wife for your husband, your hopes for your marriage, and worthwhile memories of your history together.

Have you noticed how everyone brings gifts to the Bride and Groom but most of the time the Bride and Groom don't give gifts to each other? That is simply not right, since it is both their wedding day.

This is why your journal is called a MOG/Husband Journal, because it will be given to your Mighty Man of God, your Godly Husband as a Wedding Gift. For those already married you will give this to your husband on your anniversary. This is the best gift you could offer him other than yourself. Why is that? The journal tells him that he had your heart long before you ever met while you were single and for you wives, it's another private way of sharing your heart with your husband. Your journal will give him added security in your relationship, because you kept your mind, heart and emotions within these pages and saved it all for him and not given to another, showing you're trustworthy and that there is no one else for him to compare himself too. What a pretty powerful concept, huh?

God doesn't just bless one without blessing the other; mutual blessing is what God always sets out to accomplish. So, how does giving your MOG journal to your husband bless you? The more intimate and honest you are within your journal pages the more your husband will be allowed to get to know the real inner you.

If you shared in your writing about some deep experiences, he may recognize your mood changes to match those written in your journal, so that he will know how to comfort and love you during the current situations that pop up in your life. Give up the myth of having a husband that can read your mind and give him a chance to read your heart in your journal! So, do your homework and see it as a blessing!

Homework:

First, you completed the Commitment Ceremony by committing yourself to God.

Single Princess:

The next thing to do and is your most important homework assignment is to begin journaling. It is imperative that you are consistent with your journal writing throughout your commitment in believing for the Man of God. That doesn't mean you have to write daily, simply when you feel inspired to do so. Please follow the instructions given that best work for you. Remember the more you slack off from journal writing the more hindered you will be in your quest of preparing yourself and meeting your Man of God. Therefore, the likelihood of you settling for less than God's best for your life.

To get started you must purchase a journal that is strictly to be used to write to your Godly Husband to be. In selecting a journal find one that either reflects you, your personality, favorite color, etc. or one you think will be attractive to the Man of God's eye.

How do you write to someone when you don't know who it is or what their name is? Excellent question! You don't address him by name. Depending on how your heart is feeling and how ready you are to having a relationship will help you decide how to acknowledge him.

This is definitely not for someone still so full of hurt from a previous relationship and wants to "man-bash". Remember we're talking about princes, Godly Men. So, if you're still that hurt then you will not receive healing from writing to your MOG. Instead use your journal for personal discovery and healing. Read the book, do the homework with the goal of your healing in mind. Then return to writing to him when you're healed enough to start believing God for your Godly mate.

Here are some examples:

Dear Brother - Usually means I have accepted the fact that God has someone for me so I am doing this out of obedience, but I'm not that crazy about the idea...yet. It could mean that you are in a friendlier mood and just wanted to talk to whom God has for you out of a more companion/friend state of mind.

Dear Man of God – Can mean I am stating who you are and who you will be in our relationship. I am learning to receive you as such, as I learn to submit to your authority within the relationship. Calling him a Man of God (MOG) is a reminder not to settle for less than a Man of God. It can be seen as a progressive way of improvement from calling him "Brother" to recognizing the idea of him having a closer level to your heart than you were ready to admit before.

Dear (My) Mighty Man of God – Signs of becoming less fearful in acknowledging him and beginning to warm up to the idea of using terms of endearment.

Dear Sweetheart, Darling, Honey, any loving nickname...etc. – You're ready and more comfortable to share and open to revealing your heart onto paper and to him. This is where real healing; self-discovery and Godly revelation can begin.

Questions you would ask me if we were face to face...

Q. Why do you suggest for me not to address my journal writing to the boyfriend I have now?

A. You do not know how this relationship will turn out. Keep and guard your heart, save truly intimate secrets only for your husband. He will love you the more for it and you will be glad you did, too. Imagine sharing all of this addressed to your current beau, only to discover that he is not your God chosen mate for your life. How do you explain this journal to your husband? What about the gift you were going to give him on your wedding day to be used to bless you both? And if this current boyfriend (I am trusting that he is a Man of God; otherwise you wouldn't give him the time of day), ends up being the Godly spouse for you, he will appreciate all that you saved for him while you were courting and still cherishes the gift you gave. You can't lose this way.

Q   How do I write to him?

A.   Write to him in the way you would talk to him. Be yourself. Do not be startled if while writing you notice yourself writing things or using vocabulary you're not accustomed to saying. Why is this? I learned that as I wrote to my Mystery Prince that clichés, vocabulary or even my writing style changed. I asked God about this and his reply made a lot of sense. He told me, "As you know, men and women communicate differently. You're writing words that he would say, allowing him to understand when he reads your heart."

Q.   What do I write? How do I get started?

A.   Here are a couple of ideas. Introduce yourself if you want, this isn't necessary since he will be receiving this on your wedding day; it's up to you. Record the date and time - Then you can measure how much you have changed and grown when you read your journal later on. Ask him questions you are dying to know about him. What are his favorite things? How did he find Jesus? Share about what is currently going on in your life, how you're feeling, whether good, bad, indifferent or about some upcoming decisions you have to make. Write down some Bible verses, favorite quotes, and things God is showing you, events, etc.

Q.   Is there anything else you suggest or that I need to know?

A   Keep your journal with you in your purse, book bag, as long as it is near you. Why? For two reasons, one, it eliminates you worrying if someone found it and read your intimate thoughts and two, whenever you're inspired to write, it is at your fingertips. When inspired to write, do not procrastinate, trust me, you will regret it. You might miss the most important thing you really needed to share with him or you are delaying the inevitable healing you need to move on.

If you find yourself crying as you write, remember that is good, healthy and cleansing. It means you are being real honest with yourself, God and your husband-to-be and that the healing process is beginning. It may really puzzle you that you are crying about something you can talk about, but once you've written it you're sobbing. Why is that? The answer is simple; there is something about writing it down that is cleansing to your heart. You can talk about the topic fine because you are still "guarded" with people, but when you are "unguarded" with yourself on paper your writings become like a mirror, a reflection you can't run or hide from. Then you are allowing yourself to confront some issues and allowing God to bring in revelation to restore and heal you. Whatever you do, don't avoid this; this is what truly prepares you to love yourself and to begin to be ready to love someone else. When you see how broken you were and didn't even know it and knowing God loved you anyway, makes you fall deeper in love with Him. Once you are in love with Him and the real you, then you can be ready to fall in love with the real heart of the prince chosen for you. Amen? Amen.

Q.   Other than journal writing, what else do you suggest I do?

A.   Pray for your Man of God. This is the most important thing you can do for him and your future relationship. Ask God to reveal his needs to you. Still don't know how to pray, what to say or how to start? I suggest for you to buy the book, The Power of a Praying Wife, by Stormie Omartian. In her book, the table of contents has a list of selected topics to pray over him. This powerful book really works!

Chapter 3

How Long Will It Take?

You need to calm down and don't be in a hurry. Haven't you heard the song that says? "You can't hurry love. No you just have to wait. Love don't come easy. It's a game of give and take." That song was written by Lamont Dozier, and brothers, Brian and Eddie Holland, originally performed by The Supremes and later Phil Collins. It is so fitting and very true. You're learning through your journal writing how to give and take while healing.

Something else to remember is that everyone is different. How ready you are will be depend on you. How you meet your Man of God will be uniquely different compared to others. When you meet him may be sooner or later than your friends. Whatever you do, "Do not compare yourself to them or compare your marriage to someone else's." This is a strategy of Satan to discourage you. To get you to think, "What is wrong with me? Why does she have someone in her life and I don't? Why is their marriage better than mine?" You don't know what she has been through in her personal life or hasn't been through compared to your experiences. God could have dealt with her regarding all her issues and therefore, she is now ready for the next step regarding courting or within her marriage. Where you are in this process, is where you should be focusing your attention.

I like to think of your journey (whether single or married) and compare it to an analogy of running laps around a track. For example, no one is better than you, or worse than you, not above or below, not faster or slower than you. The only difference is distance and time. How far we have to run on the track of life and healing from our issues and experiences are based on how much we had to deal with. A quick 100-yard dash for one person may be equivalent to being their first love and praise God they waited for the Godly Love Match of their life. Whereas, those that have had broken relationships one after another have harder hearts, trust issues, etc. They have more laps to run. Now, time is the other factor. You may only have to run a 100-yard dash, but if you're not interested in a relationship and just linger until you get to the finish line that is fine. If you want a relationship and have a list of things to be healed of, then pick up the pace. You need to take your journal writing, your relationship with God and others more seriously to prepare you for your God encounter with the Man of God. It all is based on your pace.

Do not think I don't know how you feel, because I do. You may believe that I already have My Mighty Man of God due to the dedication page at the front of this book. Well, I don't as of yet. (smile) I'm in the process even as I type this to you. I have done more laps than anyone I know. When God had me first minister this to someone I thought, "Oh, what a good idea." Then later He would direct me to whom to share this with. After sharing it for the third time, I was praising God for using me yet again. Then He pointed out that this message was for me, too. I wasn't remotely interested in taking my own medicine. I wrote in a journal out of obedience to God not to deal with issues, not to heal, and most definitely not to have hopes of preparing for a man, let alone a Godly Man. This

WHEN YOU'RE READY FOR THE FAIRYTALE

tells you I had a lot of laps to go before I even got started.

Well, I watched what God was doing in the lives of those He had me minister this message to and I began to notice significant changes in them. They became more confident, then stages of their personal development were more apparent and finally the right Godly spouses entered their life. That's when I said, "Hey! I'm doing the same thing. What did they do to get someone as wonderful as that to love and treat them like that?" The only thing different I noticed about them and me was they finished their journal. Once they wrote the last page, (of their 1st journal) and closed the book. Poof! Their God chosen mate entered their life. I was so excited for them and focused on my own journal writing.

I dreamily imagined as soon as I'd finished with my journal my awesome Man of God would appear, too! As my last few pages of my journal were drawing close, I became nervous. Any day I would be finished with my journal meant any day I would be meeting him. I was so excited but terrified all at the same time. I would purposely write long entries one day and then drag out writing sentences on others to stall for time. Then I finally finished my journal. I slammed the journal shut. Poof! I looked around; I waited and looked some more. Nothing! I became disheartened and went to God. "Why didn't this work for me but for the others?" He wisely replied, "It will when you finally start being real (honest) in your journal instead of all the fluff you're writing of what you think he wants to read and what you're willing to tell. Start another journal."

You don't want to hear those words, so learn from me and from the beginning. Those that finished their journals it took them about one year from the time I told them of God's instruction to write in their journals and to allow God to take care of the rest. One special friend of my mine that heeded this message it took her two years of journal writing, but she has her prince and I went to the wedding. It took them only one journal and one to two years later. Poof!

As for me? Well, obviously, no 100-yard dash for me, I have had a list of my own issues to be healed from, but I am so encouraged everyday, because of the healing I have already experienced. I am more confident than I have ever been in my life. I'm more honest with others and myself than I have ever been. This encourages me because with each passing day I am that much closer to meeting him. I know what you're thinking. That's great and all, but how long has it taken you? I'm going on fifteen years and nearly twenty journals later. The time that's required to be properly prepared whether it be for me, my mighty Man of God and our romance just tells me how much sweeter the romance will be and I am at the point I don't want to rush a thing, I want it all! I want the entire Fairytale! I have seen others have it; I want you to have it and so does God. So, don't get wrapped up in how long it takes, get lost in how good it is going to be!

So do your homework!

I recall I was so stubborn about submitting to the idea of having to write in a journal to a Man of God that I spitefully told God, "Fine, I'll buy the ugliest journal I can fine at the $1 Store!" I went to the $1 Store to do just that, only to discover they were all out of journals. If you have ever visited the $1 Store you know that they are NEVER out of journals. I even considered buying post-it notes just to get started but I was too fearful of God to dare. I ended up in Wal-Mart for something and decided to look for a journal and found my first journal there. When I look at other people's journals and they are so nice, elegant, etc. I don't feel any less about my cheaper journal. You know why? My journal represents me and where I was and what I was experiencing at the time I bought it. I wouldn't change my journal for anything! It's me and we all need to be content, meaning that there isn't anything about us we would change or even want to change unless it is for the better. Just like our testimonies, never forget where you have been and where you have come from. Your journal will remind you of those places.

Homework:

Prayerfully invite God to help you with this assignment. Then write a list of traits and characteristics you want your Man of God to have, those you don't want him to have, and those you are willing to compromise on. Remember he is the "Right" Man not the "Perfect" Man.

Singles: I don't think it's fair to expect perfection when we ladies are far from it ourselves. Another note to keep in mind, if you write down an unrealistic list, this could delay the process. I have known God to deal with the list maker only to have them come back and re-write the list.

Wives: You've married your husband and know more insightful things than the single ladies. What issues or strongholds does your husband struggle with? Those he rather not talk about? Things you've discerned and God has revealed to you of his past? Things that hinder your closeness? Make a list of what you want to see changed, pray over your husband and these items in your journal. Invite God to get involved in them and Believe God for the outcome and document it in your journal the date and situation when the victory came!

This assignment is crucial. Don't believe me? Singles, this list is what is going to save and protect your heart. I'll prove it to you. Many women and even girls have ideas of who their Dream-Man's qualities would be. However, this list is kept in their minds and when their emotions and loneliness nags at them, once a good-looking, available bachelor crosses their path they mentally run through this list. If he comes close to half or most of the desired qualities they settle for him and get hurt and end up miserable. Why? They justified in their mind that it is better to toss the list than be lonely, because who can really stack up to the standard they created, nobody's perfect. They believe this because there is some truth mixed with a lie to convince them of this. The only truth to this is that nobody is perfect. Having a standard is what will save and protect your heart and God does have someone who matches it, because He knows you and the desires of your heart as well as your Man of God's. He made you both with each other in mind. Read Psalms 37:4 and Matthew 6:33.

Wives, learning to write these things in your journal is learning how to Love your husband in another way called, "covering your husband" of his shortcomings, keeping his heart safe and protecting his reputation. By writing it down instead of sharing with a girlfriend and truly giving it to God in full surrender while you pray for him and his issues.

Keep your mind and heart steady on your relationship

with the Lord. As you read your Bible and recognize your short comings and learn how to make the necessary changes in order for your life to line up and follow the right way to live, based on what the Bible says, you become a better person and life becomes easier to live. Now transfer that same mind set to your journal. Your journal has the standard written in it as to how the Man of God should line up and his life should follow your created checklist. If a bachelor that approaches you doesn't line up with the list, you dismiss his advances without a thought or hesitation. You just saved your heart from any temptation and aggravation. With a husband, all you can do is be patient and pray. Then thank God for knowing the difference and the wisdom He granted you to guard your heart to ward off the wrong suitor or to not be discouraged when nothing appears to change with your husband. This would prove to be a teachable moment between Daddy and His daughter, as He smiles at you for making the right choice of standing your ground through it all.

(NOTE: Reality Check – After making a list of preferred qualities, ask yourself could you honestly measure up and say the same about you? Be reasonable and make sure most of the characteristics are traits and not all physical attributes.)

DAPHNE M. HUNTER

Chapter 4

Being Encased Like a Rose

Reading this chapter's title, I am sure the Disney Movie, 'Beauty and the Beast' came to mind. I didn't intend for that; however, it is a perfect illustration of what I am to describe. I mean we are talking about fairytales so it proves to be fitting.

Imagine yourself as the Rose. The rose is not to be touched, spoken to, or manipulated. It is encased for a reason. Onlookers do not understand why this rose is encased nor are they at liberty to free this rose. This rose is submitted under the authority and functions at the whim of the Master that the rose is entrusted to. Our perspective of this Master is based on the outlook the rose chooses.

Who is this Master? The Master is Almighty God, Himself. When we entered this commitment and decided to trust Him by giving Him full control of our most personal area of our lives, our love life. He took us at our word and encased us, for protection from ourselves and from others. We are frail, weak and tired of making poor choices and ready to have given up on all hope. So, He took us, set us apart for His work and for the work He needs to do within us for our own good. He wants to do work through us to make a difference to others (this is the only contact we have with others through our glass case).

When you are enclosed within this case, no one realizes or even notices that you are encased. Although, there is a sure way of knowing when you have been encased. How do you know you're encased? You go about your business, perhaps a daily routine and one day you realize no one notices you "romantically". You start to wonder, when was the last time someone looked at you in a flirtatious way? When was the last time you were complimented by a man, or about your hair, dress or when you've done your makeup differently? As you realize no one has, not for a while or it's been a long time, you think that something is wrong you. So, you start looking for such compliments and when they don't come you finally feel and recognize the glass case you're enclosed in. You see them, but they somehow don't see you, you just exist. You want to fight against its entrapment, desiring to be noticed, but tired from your fight you accept the fact that no one even notices your struggle. The sooner you give up this fight the better for you and the quicker you move onto the healing process. It doesn't feel like it but there are more important things to focus on, which is exactly what happens. When the reality sets in that it is only you within this case and that no one can sense this separation but you, nor would they understand it if you tried explaining it you realize there is no use but to accept it. That's when you begin to focus on dealing with the issues you have been avoiding all this time. This process takes time, and the time depends on the number of issues and severity of the pain experienced. Remember the laps around the track analogy?

Believe it or not, the day comes that enough healing has transpired within you that no more can be done through your glass enclosure. The next phase of your healing requires the aid of others.

You will not know of the appointed time when the Master chooses this; however, you will recognize its effects.

Personally, I recall the day my encasement was over. I felt the difference the day I felt exposed. To my surprise, I craved to be enclosed as if I were reaching to pull the glass back over me. Then I was met with God's reassurance, "Its okay, Baby Girl. You're ready, you can handle it." I didn't feel like I could handle it, in fact, I didn't even want to. It is ironic the one thing you fight to escape from is the one thing you long for. It wasn't long before I was the target for advances from worldly men, seeing and even sensing their gazes made my flesh crawl. I felt "icky". I later was "seen" by Christian brothers, I felt more at ease recognizing the difference, there was more peace, and their gaze was more comfortable as they as well as I knew our boundaries. It was the first time I felt safe among men. I truly appreciate my Godly brothers and their role as Sons of God. I once shared this with a true MOG brother of mine and he was pleased knowing the difference his presence made.

So, you too will know when your encasement is over the moment your beauty is appreciated by the opposite sex. It will come as a surprise to you after going so long without a single look your way. Then as others take notice you will start wondering when did this happen that they even noticed. What did I do differently that caught their attention? Nothing, it's just your time to be revealed. Not because you're healing is completed because it is not. It just means that you are not so "guy crazy". God is and has been the number one Man of your life. He can now trust you not to be distracted by just any guy.

Homework:

1. Now knowing what it means to be "encased" share your story. Just so you know wives can feel encased, too. Have you ever felt like your husband no longer sees you, compliments you, etc. If other men notice you especially when your husband doesn't, what do you do to ward this attention off and dismiss the haunting thoughts that resurface later?

2. In the story, 'Beauty and the Beast', the rose was a gift and so are you. Life is a gift from God and we should never take this gift for granted. Obviously, this gift is precious to us, as we desire to give it and share it with the Man of God. To get use to the idea of everyday being a gift from God, obtain a devotional book or calendar. Whether you purchase one or sign up for a free devotion to be emailed to you daily, make a point to spend time with God as you reflect and appreciate this gift, your life.

I made a deal with God not to read the devotion in advance but wait until that actual day arrived. So that flipping the page was like the unwrapping of a gift. Making every day feel like Christmas to me. What is more powerful is that each day the devotion became prophetic. It helped me in my journal writing, as I would write about my expectations and what that devotion meant to me, as I would share it with my Man of God.

Chapter 5

In Love with Jesus

I've heard of people speaking of being in love with Jesus, but I couldn't understand or even imagine it. Actually at first it seemed so sacrilegious to me. How can you think of your Lord and Savior that way, as a man? But that is what He was and is all God and all Man.

In the same way, I had heard people say that Jesus had been tempted in all the ways we have and that He knows and understands all that we experience. I couldn't accept that. I never heard about Him being tempted by women. I thought of God too pure for that. Then I thought of how compassionate Jesus was, how pure and beautiful His heart was and then His teachings. With His whole being exuding God of course people would be drawn to Him like a magnet, especially women. A man that validated women in a time no one had. Yeah, I'm sure the temptation was there, if not for Him definitely for the women, having never heard or met a man such as Him.

Then I remembered one of my earliest little girl fantasies. I was not even five years old when I said I wanted to grow up and marry Jesus. I was afraid to tell adults or even other kids, as they would laugh at me and think I was silly or worse...weird. It was about 15 years ago that I had my first experience of falling in love with Jesus. I was spending all my spare time in His Word, praying to Him, thinking of Him, singing to Him, so much so that I felt His presence hover near me. I became giddy, had butterflies in my stomach and all the effects of falling in love. I remember how good I felt for days and that I never wanted it to end. I was afraid to tell anyone just like I had as a little girl. Finally, I spoke to my aunt about how great my relationship was with God and she asked me, "The way you feel about God, does it feel like you're in love?" Embarrassed but truthful, I admitted, "Yes, it does." "She told me how she fondly remembered when once she had that and missed that feeling." Then it hit me, "You have felt that before, too?" I was relieved to know I wasn't weird since I wasn't the only one to have felt that, but then again I felt a little disappointed not to be the only one to know my Jesus this way. Then I focused on how great His presence felt and that He loves everyone and I wanted everyone to feel as good as I did. I even wondered how long would being in love with Him last. Therefore, I learned it is possible to fall in love with Jesus and your love grows for eternity if you work at it, just like all relationships do if you're willing.

1Looking back now from the time I was a wee little girl to now I had no idea how in love I would truly be with Him. Now I can say that I am very happily married to Him since having my own spiritual wedding day five years later in 2006. I can't even imagine my life without Him. I'm completely sold out to Him, I want to please Him, serve Him more than anything else. I can honestly say I am at a point in my life that I am completely fine with being single for the rest of my life, because as long as I have Him, which is for an eternity, I have everything I need, want and could hope for.

The only reason I journal now is for continued revelation, healing and because He tells me to, not so much for the Man of God; although, I know he is coming.

To be honest, I am not in search of the Man of God like I once was. I am only a lady in waiting for him, because it is God's Will for me to marry. That's a big difference from where I had been. In the beginning I started writing in my journal out of obedience because God told me to. As I was healing, I wanted a relationship and the Man of God to show up so badly and thought I was ready and really was not. Praise God for His wisdom and timing. I was writing to the Man of God entreating both God and him to show up until the last few years.

Now I am not even remotely interested in the Man of God showing up because I have had it so good with just my Lord. In fact, so much so, that I have developed another fear, the fear of transference. Once you have the best relationship with the Perfect Man, Jesus, how do you go from perfect to imperfect? Not hardly fair to the Man of God. Sounds like a set up for disappointment and who needs that after all one has been through? Maybe that is the point. To have a relationship so good with God that once the Man of God steps into the picture there is no comparison or no competition to God, that He knows you won't replace Him once the other man enters your life. This is how you still have your needs met by a Savior, when a husband can't meet them. You wouldn't want to put undue pressure or unrealistic expectations on a fallible man. How unfair is that to him or to you? So, simply fall in love with Jesus.

Maybe you still don't know how to fall in love with Jesus. Perhaps if you would allow yourself to just believe this version of a story I've told myself in how I see Jesus as the ultimate lover it won't be so difficult to keep yourself pure for Him.

Are you familiar with the story of Cyrano de Bergerac? Or the modern day re-telling of the movie, Roxanne, with Steve Martin? It's a story about a man that is ashamed of his physical appearance but falls in love with this extremely beautiful woman and he wants to woo her. Imagine you are this woman and Jesus is this man. He observes you from afar, he knows every detail about you, he enjoys your smile, your laugh, listening to you sing when others aren't there, the way you talk, how you dress, he is completely mesmerized by you, but too shy and too much of a gentleman to approach you. He is in the background, in the shadows. He goes unnoticed by you, whereas other more boisterous men who are less chivalrous are vying for your attention, causing Him to step aside. It grieves Him as he witnesses these men act less chivalrous and their ill treatment towards you, and yet He waits to see how you respond to these fellows. You are physical attracted to one such man that catches your eye. This further grieves Him as He knows He is no competition to the natural shell of a man, all He has to offer is all His heart, where it is very clear this other man has none. Yet He waits with hope.

Jesus is lovesick for you and will do anything to win your heart. He is captivated by your beauty. He decides to send his heartfelt words to woo you through love letters, just to have his love delivered to you. These sincere loving words penetrate to your inner core of your heart and you fall for Him instantly. You yearn for more of His sincere poetic words to warm you, as your and His love for each other is pure and true. However, you long for more than the satisfaction of His words, but crave a relationship with him, so you invite him and He responds. You no longer fall for those shallow, empty men without a heart but have learned the value of a steadfast, loving heart of a truly strong natured man where the outside appearance is no longer relevant. As soon as you are united, it's not long before you both have to part and yet he still sends his love to her through another.

After reading that paragraph do you see Jesus? Do you see how much He loves you? He is so captivated by you and no other.

He delivers His love letter to you through His words in someone else's handwriting as to protect His identity but still offer you His heart, in what's called a Bible. When He can't be with you, His heart aches for you that He sends the Holy Spirit to comfort you while you are apart. Knowing the Holy Spirit can only tell you what he is told, as Jesus says, "Tell her…" Jesus further encourages your heart to hold on to hope of Him one day returning to come back for you, His true love as He promises there will be a day that you will be reunited. So not to have you discouraged, He excites you with the promise of preparing a place for you and Him to reside and be together forever.

With a love like that, how can you not wait on Him? Have you ever experience such a genuine love like that from anyone else here on Earth? I think it's safe to say…No. When you finally see how much you are valued and thought about and that you have a love like that already, settling for less is no longer an option. Trust me; falling in love with Jesus is so worth it!

Want another scenario? The previous one and this one helps me stay in love with Jesus and gives me the strength to ward off any imposter that isn't the Man of God that has been sent for me. I imagine Jesus as my husband, that He loves me so deeply, tenderly and unconditionally. A love like no one else could possibly understand. A love that was so true that it cost Him His life to defend me. In order to protect me and what we have, he was taken and killed on my behalf and now I am left here, a widow.

So that you can understand what I mean, imagine this: One day my love and I go on a romantic walk. While chatting we are interrupted by some mean-spirited scoundrels who take turns shouting indecent and offensive accusations about me to Him. In my utter embarrassment and humiliation, I try to convince Him to ignore them, as I tug at His arm encouraging Him to walk the other way, but He refuses. Why? He is determined not to allow anyone to speak of His Bride this way. Although, flattered by His chivalry, I begged Him to ignore their words as my shame ate at me knowing all the grotesque accusations were unfortunately true. I hated for Him to have to find out. Now that His life was threatened for sticking up for my honor, in which I had none, I knew there was no honor in having a dead husband killed to save a reputation I never truly had. How could I let my husband be killed to defend me, a sinful woman with the kind of past I had. My love believing only the best of me, believing me to be so innocent, that He loved me so much to never believe such horrid stories of me and was willing to give up His life to prove otherwise. His belief of me was a lie. Although, my past and shame had caught up to me and I would do anything to cover it up, it wasn't worth losing the Love of my life, my Husband. That this time as I pulled on His arm, I whispered in his ear, "Don't. Don't do this, for all they said is true. I'm guilty. I've sinned so badly and done all that they said." Tears, shame, humiliation all streaked my face and to my amazement He so lovingly looked into my eyes and gently replied, "I know." My mouth gaped in awe and disbelief. Then why would He dare put Himself in such peril? His loving eyes said it all, it's because He still found me worthy to fight for, all the while knowing of what I had done. I had never known such love. They had beaten Him so badly, determined to kill Him so horribly and hung Him to make a public spectacle. As He hung there and looked down at me with me looking up at Him, our eyes communicated all our love and it was understood. His love would never leave me and He would go on and wait until I joined Him.

As I mourn him not being here in the natural, I am still comforted in my heart by His presence that never leaves me, reminding me of the strength of His love for me. It is this strength that brings me joy enough to bring a smile to my face as I recall our moments of intimacy enjoyed in conversations, while singing, while dancing, etc. No one can take that away from me. He looks after me, a widow and will take care of my children, the orphans. I will continue to go on waiting until He releases me to marry and He will let me know when He sends that special someone to stand in His stead until the day we are finally reunited.

Do you see Jesus, now? Could you wait for a love that loves you that much? It increases the value of His love, doesn't it? Therefore, it increases the value of you, too.

Homework:

Answer these questions and write them in your Journal.

1. Have you ever fallen in love with Jesus? How do you feel about this question? Can you fall in love with Him now after reading those two scenarios? Which scenario really spoke and touched you?

2. In your opinion, what makes a romance a fairytale?

3. What do you want your fairytale to be?

4. What makes a fairytale a fairytale to you?

5. Watch the original animated Disney Movie, *"Cinderella"* and take notes of any insight this movie gives you about fairytales, your fairytale or any spiritual insight. Also, include what you believe makes the story, Cinderella a fairytale, and what this story means to you.

6. Read the book of Esther (in the Bible) once through.

Chapter 6

Learn From Cinderella

Like most girls, I love fairytales. Cinderella is one of my favorites, but the reason Cinderella earned a place in this book is because the story kept resurfacing as I was writing in my journal and believing God for my Mighty Man of God. When I decided to finally pay attention, God gave me great insight into this fairytale to give me hope in believing for a fairytale of my own. That is why Cinderella will now be used to encourage you in your journey of your unique fairytale.

I believe God is always talking and revealing His insights to us in all things. So, I will purposefully be dissecting The Walt Disney animated version of Cinderella in the order in which it is shown. Be sure to pay close attention to the words spoken or sang.

During the opening song, I felt the song substantiates that we all are princesses. For instance, saying that the throne is the proper place for us to be. In fact, the Bible supports this with the verses found in Ephesians 2:6 and Revelation 3:21. Once you're ready, give your heart a chance and it will lead you to romance. Your heart definitely needs time to heal in order for it to dare venture out to lead you to that special encounter with your very own prince. But once it does, your dreams will unfold into the sweetest story ever told. Ready, princess?

As already depicted for you, everything starts with

the Kingdom. This establishes your identity, your boundaries and the authority placed over you. As this kingdom is described to being one that is rich, peaceful, prosperous, believes in romance and tradition, it is safe to say so is the one of our Heavenly Father. This is further upheld in the scriptures when we are taught that God is a God of abundance, more than enough, that He is Jehovah Jireh our provider. Jesus is our Prince of Peace; He gives us peace that surpasses all understanding. It is this peace that aids us while we endure the wait for our Man of God. Out of our faithfulness to serve our King everything we touch and do will prosper. While we focus on the King and building His kingdom he will grant us the desires of our hearts by presenting us to our Mighty Men of God. The good news is He wants us to be united with our prince even more so than we do, so we can't lose as long as we don't lose sight of our relationship and service to the King. Later on in future chapters you will get a sense of how romantic God truly is, no one can write a love story like He can. Following God isn't about traditions; however, He does have principles that will bless us should we choose to follow them.

As Cinderella's father was devoted to her, imagine how much more our God is to us, His daughters. If we have such favor with one, then we are highly disfavored by another. In this instance, Cinderella suffered mistreatment by her stepmother. Our enemy is mean, jealous, bitter and looks for every opportunity to persecute, abuse and humiliate us every chance he gets through those we have relationships with. We are not to retaliate with evil, but do good. (Romans 12:17) Regardless of their hateful words or deeds we are to repay them with gentleness, kindness, and be hopeful despite the circumstances. (Galatians 5:22 and 1 Corinthians 13:7) How do you do this? Keep the faith by singing and keep believing that your dreams will come true. (Hebrews 11:1) The best songs to sing are praises to our King and remember to keep His promises before your eyes. (Psalm 103:2)

Cinderella actually displays characteristics that we should make an effort to acquire if we are not already demonstrating them. Go ahead and take personal inventory of yourself as I explain the significance of each trait.

It appears that Cinderella does not complain, murmur or mumble regardless of the reality of her monotonous routine day after day. This reduces the drama experienced in her life. She lives up to the Proverbs 31 Woman. Check that out in the Bible. She keeps a positive outlook, as she is not dwelling on her situation, she simply moves on to the next task required of her.

Cinderella is very friendly, thoughtful and quite hospitable (even to mice). Recall how she treated the new mouse, Gus? She had clothes for him, but called him a visitor, and greeted him warmly. Just like God, she adopted this mouse like He adopted us. For example, she gave him a home, a name, a family, told him of the rules of the house, gave him food and warned him of his enemy, Lucifer. These are definitely characteristics of our God and King and should be of the House of God that we call a church home.

No one treats your home as well as you do. This is very clear by the lack of involvement with the stepmother and stepsisters. Cinderella is made a servant in her own home, which would appear so cruel but it actually proved to be to her benefit. Serving teaches you, prepares you and humbles you. You will know your place and position if you start at the bottom, what may feel like humble beginnings will be used to promote you.

Just because Cinderella is mistreated doesn't mean she is necessarily a doormat. She still treats everyone with love whether they deserve it or not. When she speaks to Lucifer, the cat, she speaks firmly when needed. She still has good things to say, as she tells Bruno, the dog, to look on the bright side of every situation including when it came to Lucifer. Another way of saying, love your enemies. She also says, "I mean there must be something good about him", so look for the positive in others. Even though Lucifer was a trouble-maker, he tries to tempt you in order to destroy you, as he did with the mice when they were seeking food. Lucifer was a green eye monster and deceiver. Yeah, that sounds about right, just like the enemy we have to deal with now in our lives.

Cinderella is quite graceful, poised, with proper posture and balance. She speaks to each person in the morning and when she was falsely accused, she never defended herself although she was innocent. Whereas her accuser, her stepmother, quickly sides with Cinderella's opposition, she does not offer to hear both sides, but is quick and mean in her judgment and her sentence is immediate. The only hope that we can receive from experiencing such situations is to remember her response, just like Jesus, He trusted God with the results. If you are facing extraordinary problems and are suffering from extraordinary punishment, then it's all a set-up for a breakthrough experience around the corner. Don't believe me? What was happening while Cinderella was enduring all of this? The king was scheming, planning and desiring for the prince to get married.

What did the king, the prince's father (and remember yours too,) say he wanted? He felt his child had grown up, matured and now was distant so he desired for him to remain at home. Then he wanted to have grandbabies, to hear the pitter-patter of feet in the palace. He didn't just want his son married just to anyone but someone who would make a suitable wife and mother. He wanted his son to experience the very best romance and decided to help by having the Ball. The king was clever as he had a reasonable explanation for the timing of such an event; therefore, allowing him to create the right atmosphere and able to dismiss any objections from his son. I especially appreciate that the king was not arrogant or pompous as his invitation went out to all eligible maidens; all were equals in his sight.

Meanwhile as Cinderella is still working she is singing through her troubles, which makes the work not so bad. It kept her heart light, hopeful as she refused to dwell on her problems. All of this equipped Cinderella not to be just a servant, but a homemaker and ultimately a good wife and mother material. While you are keeping busy, Lucifer tries to make things worse, more work for us, to keep us distracted and discouraged into believing that our current situation will never end. Until that knock on the door comes, our opportunity, our chance meeting is presented right in front of our face. Nothing Lucifer does can stop what the King has sent our way. A letter, an invitation was sent from the king to Cinderella. That letter is true for you; it's called your Bible. Just like how that king's letter made it to Cinderella's house, the promise and plan of God for your life is going to make its way to your house because God knows where you are and He knows how to get it to you. He is not limited to the ways you know about. He has plenty of ways to deliver what is meant for you.

Cinderella's stepsisters are the example of how not to be. They are simply ugly inside and out, they are mean, rude, have no manners, are argumentative, vain, gossip, snobby, jealous, selfish, fake, antagonists, and have no compassion. Did you notice the reaction of the men in authority towards the stepsisters? The prince rolled his eyes at them, the king shrieked at them and the Grand Duke wasn't very impressed with them while presenting the glass slipper for them to try on. This is an example of how it may be necessary to make some changes in our fleshy attitudes. Don't lose heart, as only God can make permanent changes in us. The biggest goal is to be submissive to God in this process and it won't be so difficult to transfer your act of submission to your husband as you recognize his authority in your life. Cinderella was to live in the palace, she already submitted herself to her stepmother, so submission was easy to extend to her father-in-law the king and towards her husband the prince.

Cinderella wanted to go to the King's Royal Ball; after all she too was invited being an eligible maiden. To add to the cruelty, her stepmother gives Cinderella false hope by stating that she may go if all her work is done. Then to make sure she doesn't finish her work, the stepmother and her daughters give additional tasks for her to do.

To keep up her hope, Cinderella steals a moment to

pull out her mother's old-fashioned dress. Relying on her creativity and resourcefulness, Cinderella decides she will re-design the dress to be appropriate for the Ball. Remember princesses, you may not have much, just start with what you have right in front of you. Obviously, Cinderella is very hard working, responsible and her priorities are to put others before herself. Demonstrating this type of character, others are willing to help her out, giving her favor with all of those whose lives she has touched. When you least expect it those that you have helped along the way may just return the favor when you need it most.

As Jack and Gus collect items for Cinderella's dress they discovered a sash and some beads. Gus loudly proclaims, "Beads!" Take this as a warning to be careful about speaking your God plans to the enemy. He will try to prevent them from happening, as was the case with Lucifer and the string of beads. Cinderella simply accepts the fact that she is not going to the Ball due to her work taking so long and no time to prepare for the Ball. With dignity she keeps her head held high, although disappointed she tries to justify that the Ball wasn't going to be so...wonderful, while knowing better. Then the time came to lift Cinderella's spirits by presenting the surprise dress made for her. Unfortunately, it was short-lived as her selfish, fake, destructive step-sisters ripped her dress to shreds.

Now Cinderella is heartbroken, yet she still doesn't complain or says one negative word against them, instead, she runs out and cries. Sometimes crying is all we can do. God sees your tears. Did you know your tears are liquid prayers? Like Cinderella, we should offer our prayers in private, perhaps a special place where we can be still and quiet to hear the Holy Spirit speak to us. We may not be able to hear what is being said, due to all the damage, hurt, and trauma our heart has experienced. Feeling we can only take so much is why we no longer want to believe in our dreams anymore. Worry, doubt, and fear try to settle in and all we can do is cry as we are ready to quit on our dreams. However, when you have had it and believe you can't go on anymore is when the "unseen" steps in the picture. In Cinderella's case it was her Fairy God-Mother, in ours it's our Heavenly Father, God. The Fairy God-Mother speaks life to her as she encourages her with the words, "You're going to the Ball." These faith-filled words may sound foreign, as the circumstance looks impossible, but remember all things are possible to those that believe. Just keep on believing, and sure enough Miracles do happen. Trust me after all of this, Cinderella will and does believe in Miracles! For with God nothing is impossible.

As the Fairy God-Mother begins to work up a miracle she speaks in an unknown tongue, "Biddi Bobbity Boo". She speaks things into existence; she speaks with such faith calling those things as if they were real. For example, her turning the pumpkin into a coach, the mice into horses, turning Cinderella's rags into a gown, and created servants to serve her for a change. Now Cinderella is ready for the Ball and she looks rich. Cinderella didn't do anything to earn all of this good fortune; she simply had faith and believed. Finally, her outer appearance reflects the inner princess that she truly is. We princesses need to do the same. God is so good as not to allow one accessory to be missed or overlooked, just like Cinderella's glass slippers. It's these dainty, delicate and breakable glass slippers that end up representing the miracle, the promise and the dream Cinderella has been longing for all along. In the end, these slippers are the only manifested sign that identifies who she is and who belongs to her beloved prince.

Cinderella is so ever thankful, grateful, and appreciative as she states that this miracle is more than she could ever have hoped for. Sounds Biblical to me if you read Ephesians 3:20 which says, Now to Him who is able to do far more abundantly beyond all that we ask or think, according to the power that works within us. That power that works within us is the Power of the Holy Spirit. He's the One that maintains our hope, faith and joy while we endure our circumstances. By holding onto the promise, the dream or vision that you believe for will have to come true as long as you don't give up. Now that Cinderella is all dolled up and ready for the Ball, don't you see that this whole situation was a God set-up? Had the step-sisters not torn up her mother's dress she would have gone to the Ball looking ordinarily common as any other maiden. Cinderella would have been just as happy, but God had Bigger plans for her as He does for you, so don't settle. Don't settle for less than His perfect timing, situation and Man for you. If you wait He will make you more breathtaking and eye-catching than all others to your prince. You will be uniquely you, so beautiful and the most special woman the prince has ever been enthralled with.

Now, Cinderella is set to go to the king's palace, as she obeys the king's command to attend The Royal Ball. On her way there, the coach glows, lighting up the streets wherever it carries our princess reminding us of the light within us that shines through and the anointing upon us.

God's hand is on us as He is always in control, regardless of what the circumstances say. Cinderella's faithful serving and obedience brought her this opportunity, an open door to meet the prince. Her uncertain entrance grabs his attention and draws him to her and she is "found" and "pursued". The king is blessed and he blesses his guests as they enjoy his hospitality and through this created atmosphere the prince recognizes his bride. Even though fairytales are said not to happen in real life, they do. Our God, the King, orchestrates situations to be played out, setting us up for our fairytale love. So that not only those involved are eternally grateful for their fairytale romances, but God is thrilled to see His plan fulfilled. Truth be told, God wants your romance to happen more than you do.

One way of celebrating and rejoicing is by dancing. As Cinderella and the prince dance they discover their love and realize so this is what God had planned for them. The key to Heaven is God, His unfailing love and the love He bestows on others. Your heart has wings again causing you to be willing to trust again. With a love like this you feel as if you can fly high enough to touch every star in the sky making all things possible. The true miracle was not the material things needed to get to the Ball; it's what was missing the entire time, that special someone. Just like Cinderella, God has made a prince just for you to give you all the love you missed and so desperately needed.

Others will always try to prevent and sully God's plan for you. Stay on your guard and know this is nothing more than a feeble attempt to steal your faith, hope and love, yet again. This will continue until you win your prince and then will be an on-going battle day to day, as you fight beside him in the adventure that unfolds in your life together.

The prince almost kissed Cinderella, fortunately they didn't. This prevented them from compromising and now their first kiss was saved for their wedding day. The way it should be as Christian Men are exhorted to treat Christian Women as sisters, including their fiancée all the way until they become husband and wife. Whether or not you decide to keep your first kiss until the altar is completely up to you. Some people think this is such a little thing, but it is a big deal for those that have save that sacred first kiss, as the wait creates an even more significant meaning to them both.

During this tender moment the prince and Cinderella fall in love without knowing who the other was. Cinderella doesn't know he is the prince and the prince doesn't know her name. (Yet they were going to kiss?) At least the prince knows that she fell for him and not his title, position, or wealth. As she fled, the prince was in hot pursuit of Cinderella, and so were the grand duke and all the king's men. What does this tell you? You may very well have the love of your life right before your very eyes and still not even know it or his name. In fact, he may be just as clueless as you are. However, you dear princess are to be "found" or discovered by the prince. He will approach you. Remember his method of pursuit doesn't necessarily mean it will happen in the ways you may be expecting or are accustomed.

Although Cinderella's night is over, she is simply grateful for the experience and the memories. Having experienced a night like she had she can now endure the mistreatment awaiting her back at home. The first thing she does is immediately offer a prayer of gratitude as she thanks God for everything. Not only did that evening, her dance and the prince make an impact on her, she was made unforgettable to him as well. All they both have, as a tangible reminder of their time together was a single glass slipper. This very item was all, the king needed to do everything in his power to work on his plan for their marriage to happen. Don't worry, princesses other girls may be given the opportunity to vie for your prince but only one can fit and that's you!

How long do you have to wait for your prince? Only God knows. More important than that is the reality that it doesn't necessarily have to take a long time for the prince to be smitten with you. After that one encounter the prince already loves Cinderella, wants to marry her and is determined to find her. He even says he won't rest until he finds her; she is definitely being pursued now. The prince gives his word not only to find her, but also to marry her. This was the king's original intent, but now the prince is in agreement, as if it was the prince's idea. The king supports it, commands it and says, "So Be It!" (Amen). Then the proclamation is read throughout the land as they look for the prince's true love. God always proclaims what He is about to do before He does it. So that He is given all glory for it, as there will be no doubt that He was ultimately responsible. This will prove to be a testimony to all others to believe in Him and allow Him to take the lead in their romance as you have done. Find encouragement in Isaiah 48:3, "I have declared from the beginning the former things; they went forth from my mouth and I made them known; then suddenly I did them, and they came to pass."

Cinderella doesn't know God's plan for her love life as

she learns of the prince's feelings for her before revealing her own. Therefore, allowing her to guard her heart. Preferably, your prince will inform you of his intentions and desire to court you. However, I am very aware of several cases where God has had his darling princesses inform the princes of the King's (God's) plans for their arranged marriages according to Him.

Upon this discovery, Cinderella displays a new boldness as she recognizes that she is now loved and accepted. She is not the least worried about her status, being poor, or a servant. Instead, she sings the love song from the Ball as to rehearse her victory, to continue to hope for her dream that she has been wishing for since the beginning. What victories do you have to rehearse? Keep them before you to propel you onto the next one. As you know, while she does this, she is locked in her room. Her situation looks impossible. She's trapped! Her begging doesn't help. It looks as if she will miss her opportunity, miss the timing, and miss her prince. But victory is coming.

A trumpet sounding proves victory! It's this very same trumpet that announces the arrival of the grand duke carrying the royal proclamation of the king along with the glass slipper. It's the trumpet sound I look forward to of the true King's arrival for His bride that I'm waiting for. Either scenario, the King's Word will be established and realized. Even though others will be sent as decoys to keep the Man of God from getting to you, just keep on believing and praying. Every maiden of the kingdom is given a try to fit the slipper. Regardless of the adversity she had to experience, even while knowing that she was the one, Cinderella still waited as the other women fulfilled the king's command. Remember only she was the perfect fit for the prince as you will be for yours. You have no worries God has specifically chosen you for him and him for you. The only way to lose him is to lose hope, faith and quit because it is your faith that pulls him into your life. If Cinderella hadn't been dreaming of happiness for as long as she had, the prince would not have crossed her path. If she quit, all will be lost. If you quit on believing the promise of the prince, the Devil wins.

There is only one Cinderella, but many obstacles and opposition. Her stepmother locked her in, her stepsisters attempt to steal her man and Lucifer, the cat prevents her from receiving her key to her freedom. That is just like Lucifer. She commands him with authority, "Let Him Go!" (Regarding, letting Gus loose, the mouse, with the key.) We must speak as boldly to Lucifer as she did. When he resists, she recalls Bruno, the dog and remembers Bruno's dream of catching Lucifer one day. Bruno's one day arrived and came to pass. This is significant because as you build or cause other people's dreams to happen God will build and deliver your dreams to you! God is a God that wants to see all His children blessed, so always be thinking of what you can do for others. The blessing will be returned to you, perhaps when you need it the most. Lucifer is not only defeated, but also kicked out of the window. Sound familiar? He was kicked out of Heaven (Luke 10:18), didn't he learn his lesson?

In the meantime, not only do her stepsisters try to steal her prince but they lie and cheat as they try to force their feet to fit. No matter what extremes another may use to snatch your Man of God, God will reveal the truth. On top of that, when asked, "Are you the only ladies in the house?" The stepmother lies saying no other maidens are in the house then dismisses Cinderella as Cinderella descends down the stairs. The stepmother proceeds to mock, persecute and say obscenities about Cinderella to make her look bad. Did Cinderella care or the grand duke care for that matter? No! They both were just concerned with fitting the slipper. Thanks to her stepmother, she causes the prince's slipper to be smashed. Your promise may look broken, but God will always make sure there is provision for the vision. In this case, the other slipper was safely tucked in Cinderella's pocket. Cinderella's foot fit and therefore, the promise was kept by the prince, the king and God. It's a good thing Cinderella was prepared with the slipper right there, what if she left it in her room? We all still have our part of the responsibility in seeing the promise through, too.

Next are the wedding bells. The King is so happy to see His plan realized as intended, His son and daughter together and made one. Now he waits for multiplication of godly offspring of grandchildren to join him in the palace. Now the prince and his bride are simply enjoying their recent victory of just finding each other as they look forward to beginning their new life together. This is a start to a very bright and prosperous future. Then when you reflect on all the heartache and hardships you endured it will feel all worth it once the promise comes true. Why? It makes the promise that much sweeter.

Homework:

1. Pray for God to give you revelation as you read Esther a second time. This time take notes while reading. Write in your journal about how

Esther applies to your life and what you received from reading it.

2. Discuss similarities and contrasts of Cinderella to Esther.

3. Are there more similarities or contrasts?

4. Which one can you personally relate to more?

5. Do you see yourself as a princess more so now?

6. Which of the two stories gives you more hope?

7. Did you catch most of these insightful points as you watched Cinderella before reading Chapter 6?

8. Did you find this chapter to be insightful and enlightening?
Did you learn something new?

9. Do you see fairytales differently after dissecting the story and giving its explanation?

Chapter 7

The Esther in Us All

Have you read the story of Esther? I mean really have read it carefully? Well, if you haven't I am grateful to be the first to encourage you to do so. Should you be familiar with it, it's my hope for you to see Esther in a new light, because what you're about to learn is vital to your spiritual life and will enhance your love story. Why is it so important to recount the story of Esther? You will learn that there is a part of Esther inside of you. Let's begin to understand Esther and find out who she is and then find her in you.

In the beginning of the Book of Esther, a valuable lesson is taught to us women. That lesson is the significance of learning about place, position, authority and submission. Depending on how we decide to embrace or reject this lesson will determine the essence of our character as a woman and determines the path we take in destiny. If you choose to embrace and apply the principles, you are on your way to becoming more like Esther. Should you reject them, you may be on the "outs" like Vashti and miss the destiny you desire. I believe you chose not to be like Vashti but to be more like Esther. Notice the story doesn't begin with what to do but what not to do. Therefore, we will take a look at Vashti first. The setting is established at the king's summer's house specifically in the garden where he has decided to be extremely generous, as he displays his elaborate home and offers the best of everything to his guests. Meanwhile

Queen Vashti is conducting a separate party for the women in the palace. The point is a woman's place is beside her man. Vashti's absence at her husband's party says a whole lot. What wife allows her husband to do all the hosting? If it were only the government officials perhaps, but it's obviously not that kind of party. Look at Esther chapter 1 verse 5, it states that all were invited, the important and unimportant, sounds co-ed to me. If I were one of the unimportant guests, in awe to even be at the party I would be wondering where the queen is. I would want to see her up close. I would wonder what she would wear to such an event. Knowing I might not have a chance again.

Having a separate party shows the lack of unity between the two. There is conflict that underlines the introduction, such as notice the locations of the two parties. The king is in the garden while the queen is in the palace, a sort of upstaging the king. This further promotes the idea that the queen was haughty and more concerned about impressing her female guests than recognizing the need and request of her husband, the king, when he requests her presence to show off her beauty before his guests. She no longer respects him as neither the king nor her husband. This grieves my heart, as it is almost impossible to distinguish which of his roles is more superior. Imagine him as your husband and king. He is a truly powerful monarch of your country (a total of 127 provinces) with weighty responsibility which is awe inspiring in itself, but what about the role of husband? The man you are to allow into your heart, mind and life. The man you would want to strive to make look good to all onlookers as the kind of man other men would want to imitate and other women would hope to find. A good wife is her man's support, without the presence of support one can fall. Therefore, causing her man to appear imprudent, which later comes up for discussion among the men who disapprove of Vashti's distasteful actions. It wasn't long before the suggestion for her to be replaced was discussed.

How does this apply to us today? Ladies do not belittle your husbands. Unfortunately, we all need lessons in this area. The sooner we learn to avoid this, the better. Nowadays there are no holds barred as we lash out at each other because of our own hurt or the hurt they may inflict on us whether intentionally or not. Regardless, say goodbye to retaliation because it's not worth it in the long run. Seek the Lord and pray. Forgiveness is a better solution in order to heal and move on, then to be replaced and scarred. Belittling your husband "nips" at his heart and scars him. Once that happens he will close up and shut down and shut himself off to you and you won't get him back. In any case, allow God to work on you and him. Keeping God involved is always the answer.

Queen Vashti truly forgot who she was and where she was. She was in the palace; did she think she was "king"? Her position has now gone to her head. But who appointed her into that position? The king. Her rash refusal just bit the hand that fed her. She not only was prideful, but she selfishly forgot her role. She wasn't only representing herself. With her title and position, she represents the people of the kingdom, more specifically the women of those 127 provinces, she is the female version of the king and now she gave tasty morsels for the king's enemies to feed on. Her position to refuse to stand before the king was adamantly against him. A wife's position is to serve, assist or help her husband as long as her husband doesn't ask her to do anything against God or what His Word says. If he does ask such a thing, again seek God in prayer for His wisdom in the situation. That takes us to authority. Queen Vashti only had the authority given to her and she sabotaged it, by usurping the authority figure over her. The king, her husband is her covering, her protector and her provider. I wonder what she really thought her action would prove. Had the king done nothing what would Queen Vashti do next? Where would it stop?

As women we really have no idea of the mantle of responsibility our men have been given to take care of us, so we are to respect them for their God given roles. Respecting them is not a mere suggestion but a commandment from our Father, the King and we princesses should remember that. (See Ephesians 5:33) Our Father is the ultimate authority next is our prince. Keeping this in its proper perspective by respecting our husbands' authority, then our Daddy can protect and take care of them and us when the princes are out of order. If we don't, we wives take control (another sense of belittling our husbands), we end up weakening the men and then lose respect for them and ultimately lose them. So, let God deal with the men, it's not our place, position nor do we have the authority to correct them, we simply submit to both the authorities of God and our husbands.

I know that submission is a very touchy, sensitive subject, and that your reaction to this subject depends on your attitude. Submission does not mean you are weak; it's an actual blessing of protection. As long as you submit and something goes wrong, the blame doesn't fall on you;

however, this doesn't give us the right to be know-it-alls or say I-told-you-so. Don't you think the enemy has already done that to our princes? Keep in mind that our Men of God have strategize to slay the dragon and have been fighting the enemy in battle while away from home in the marketplace. Then that same dragon follows him home to attempt one last final blow at them before it dies and our prince steps through the door of their castle. That's when we greet them at the door with our open arms and protect their back as we sling our dagger at the dragon as we say to our husband, "Everything will be alright, God's got a plan and He is bigger than you getting it wrong. Get up, let's regroup, reason together and pray." Kind words can heal the day-to-day wounds our men take on as they fight for us in the big mean world. This will give them courage to do battle the next day and will give them the incentive to love and treat us like the princesses we want to be and are. We have to give them a reason to keep fighting and a refuge to come home to. Our submission to our husbands keeps the order of the home, keeps the men strong and will keep us happy in the long run because as the men live up to their potential we will live up to ours. As we do that, we become more tender towards them and that speaks to their hearts as this makes them feel more like a man, the kind of man they want to be for us. Queen Vashti forgot or missed all this, and by her actions she was a disappointed wife. Perhaps she felt and believed her nagging or lashing out would prove to bring change, well it did, her dethroning out of the king's heart and out of her position. Not the most popular topic, but I hope we ladies can see and meditate on the importance of place, position, authority and submission. Enough of what not to do, let's evaluate Esther and learn the areas that promoted her to becoming not only the queen in position and title, but queen of the king's heart. You might wonder if we are princesses, how are we to become a queen? Good question. While single and awaiting our prince to come, we remain a princess. Once married, we become a queen and the prince becomes a king. That's when your husband becomes the king of the castle, otherwise known as the man of the house. Don't worry because he is a Man of God, he won't lord his authority over you.

There are many obvious differences been Vashti and Esther. For example, those that consulted with the king wanted to prevent the women in the kingdom to usurp the men's authority so they suggested a woman that knew her "place" to replace Queen Vashti. Notice they wanted a woman, but they chose a "girl". I am not referring to age; I am implying that Esther was teachable to learn her place. Esther didn't enter the harem knowing what a Queen's rightful place was; she had to prepare for such a place. This should offer us all hope to learn as Esther did. How do we learn our place? You must go to the House of a King, also known as the House of God, called church. Learn the etiquette of being the princess that you are, become knowledgeable of what the King says in His House then you will apply it to your house and to your king. By belonging to the same kingdom, your prince will be learning the same things you're taught; therefore, ensuring a harmonious home of your own. Etiquette is included in your spiritual growth, as others will witness your changes in your behavior, attitude, speech, manners and dress. The longer and the more serious you are concerning your preparation for kingdom living with your Father and ultimately, for your prince, this will ensure you to enter your queenly status, resulting in impeccable character improvement. Such as, your behavior will demonstrate the following qualities that are truly becoming of a daughter of the King, they are: love, joy, peace, longsuffering (extreme patience), kindness, goodness, faithfulness, gentleness (humility) and self-control. Further practical skills can be learned as you apply these traits to serving others. A princess cannot be aloof or separated from others in the kingdom. If so, then how can she represent or be an ambassador on behalf of the King or of the people? The King's characteristics must be established within her and seen through her to verify who she is. Once the princess has been properly prepared to represent the King, her Father, she will have more opportunities to extend His Kingdom as she will serve Him and others well. In her servitude to her Father, is when a true prince in search of a true princess will recognize these attractive traits. Ladies, wait for the prince to ride in on the white horse. Don't saddle up chasing him down. Your Daddy, the King, knows where you are and He's a BIG Romantic! He'll set you up on an assignment to align you with the right prince for you. After all, don't you know that when royalty marries it's all done by arranged marriages? Your Father has it all planned out for you if you simply trust Him. That's what Esther had to do.

Since Esther exuded these qualities, her inner beauty caused her outer beauty to radiate. We, women are to strive and maintain our attractiveness, but nothing is as beautiful as a woman that spends time with the Lord, your Daddy, the King. Esther experienced favor with those in authority as she was taught her "place" under a watchful eye. This wasn't all that different from submitting to the authority of her cousin who raised her since she was an orphan.

Did you notice Esther was already conveying her understanding of place, authority and submission? All she was missing was the position. Once you have a solid relationship with your Father, the King and your loyalty is truly to Him and His Kingdom, then He can entrust you to marrying His choice prince for you. Your marriage will secure an alliance between you both and to the King and then off to fight your enemies. Only then, do you gain the position of becoming a Queen. You're a queen not just because you're married, but because you understand your place, position, authority and how to submit within your own palace; along with the kingdom qualities learned to best serve your new king, your husband. Together you both are entrusted by the King to embark on a mission, to oversee a territory and to advance His Kingdom further together. All of this preparation readies you for the adventure of a lifetime with your best life-long partner beside you; who is best equipped in your weaknesses and you are in theirs. Your Daddy, the King, knows best.

What made Esther stand out to King Xerxes, when he had a harem full of virgins to choose from? Esther's selflessness, she focused on the king rather than herself. She made it a conscious effort to think of his needs rather than her own. Her goal was to please him and in doing so she would receive great satisfaction. This won the king's admiration and he couldn't help but fall in love with her, for her heart was genuinely offered to him. This wasn't a ploy of Esther's. I believe Esther had a confidence of knowing who she was as a person and confidence is attractive. Her confidence was in knowing her God, even sensing her life's purpose was accumulating into this one moment with King Xerxes and she did the rare and unique thing, she offered herself to him rather than seeking to gain something from him. This is why the king fell in love with Esther over all the others and made her queen.

Being in the king's bedchamber or becoming the queen didn't make Esther a woman. It was the character journey as queen that I believe made Esther into a woman. Notice upon arriving to the palace, Esther was a passive, teachable girl, who learned a lot and learned very quickly. Upon her coronation she stepped into the realm of needing to be assertive. Esther kept alert and current with all dealings surrounding the palace to best support her husband's role. For example, she assisted in preventing her husband's murder, she inquired of her cousin, Mordecai's behavior outside the palace gate and recognize the timing to call a fast on behalf of her people in order to seek Godly wisdom and direction to save her people from being massacred by a schemer and granted unknowing through her own husband and king. God's favor on Esther's life allowed her the discernment to see potential problems before they materialized and she knew this. That is why she sought God for the seriousness of the undertaking of being the only influential person, let alone a woman, to save a nation whose people were spread among 127 provinces and ultimately including her. No one could do this but God.

What did Esther do? She used a tool she learned in her etiquette training from her Father God, the King, and your Daddy. She used her gentleness and humbled herself by not eating or drinking for 3 solid days and had the entire nation in agreement in unity doing the same as her. That day, Esther entered into her authority and discovered boldness, as she became the voice of her people. You having oneness like that and aligning to God's purpose, He will certainly move through such yielding as that and He did. She submitted to God. Through her humility and submission Esther displayed great strength. Esther could not have submitted when it counted if she hadn't learned it early on. Submission is a subtle, quiet strength, whereas control is obvious and boisterous. Submission and control are as different as day and night and as Esther was from Vashti. Be an Esther.

Homework:

1. Share revelation stories of what you learned from Esther.

2. Which etiquette areas do you need to work on?

3. Which level are you in...passive, assertive or authoritative?

4. How can you best use any of these levels to best support your husband (or once you're married)?

5. What did you learn most since studying Esther? Was this a new revelation or a reiteration of a truth you already knew?

6. Watch the movies entitled, One Night with the King and Esther.

7. Read Ruth and take notes.

Chapter 8

Wait Like Ruth

Waiting is never any fun regardless of the reward or circumstance. It seems especially unbearable at times where the Man of God is concerned. Remember what the Bible says in James 1:3-4 knowing that the testing of your faith produces patience. But let patience have its perfect work, that you may be perfect and complete, lacking nothing. Here's some more encouraging scriptures… Galatians 6:9 (NKJV) And let us not grow weary while doing good, for in due season we shall reap if we do not lose heart. Hebrews 10:35-39 (Message) So, don't throw it (your confidence/faith) all away now. You were sure of yourselves then. It's still a sure thing! But you need to stick it out, staying with God's plan so you'll be there for the promised completion. It won't be long now, he's on the way; he'll show up most any minute. But anyone who is right with me thrives on loyal trust; if he cuts and runs, I won't be very happy. But we're not quitters who lose out. Oh no! We'll stay with it and survive, trusting all the way. Stay and wait.

Consider this, just as you have determined not to settle for less than God's best in selecting your Man of God, you don't want the Man of God before the appointed time. You and he would be cheated out of perhaps the best part of your Godly romance. You have come this far just hold on and learn how to wait like Ruth.

I love the story of Ruth. I believe this is one of the most romantic stories of all. The Book of Ruth is proof yet again of God's faithfulness and that He is the Chief Romantic. In Ruth's story we see Godly inspiration take form in the heart of Boaz, as he will not rest to make Ruth his very own wife. Talk about a prince rescuing the princess.

Look at Ruth. What do you see? All her heart and character, not once is Ruth's physical appearance described or even mentioned. In our mind we fall in love with her and ecstatic for our heroine as we witness good things happening to the "underdog". You might call Ruth yet another Cinderella Story.

Now about Ruth... First, we learn she's a widow and can't imagine the heartache she suffered. Also being a widow herself, Naomi, her mother-in-law, decides to return to her home country, so both Ruth and her sister-in-law prepare to return to this home. What is home? It wasn't home to these two Moabite widows, only to Naomi. Home to me represents Heaven or a familiar place where you are accepted and loved or could be the heart of someone you truly belong with. To Naomi, home was to live in her own country, to be among her own people, to reside where her God resides, it became her dream to return. Sometimes you must let your dream die and let God decide if He wants you to re-visit it.

Naomi was being obedient to God to leave the world of Moab and return to the promised land of Israel. Naomi's two daughters-in-law, Ruth and Orpah, had prepared to leave with her. However, Naomi told them to stay in their own country of Moab, told them to return to their mothers and released them to remarry. Then she spoke a blessing over them stating, "May the Lord bless you as you were a blessing by your respect, commitment and service to me, to their dead husbands and to their family name."

Orpah chose to remain in Moab, while Ruth chose to stay by her mother-in-law's side. Ruth's decision to remain with Naomi is a key point, her decision to hang on meant she didn't fall for the "good" offer she wanted the perfect deal. We don't know what happened to Orpah, let's assume she did remarry. That would mean Orpah settled for a Moabite man, while Ruth would gain a prince, a man of promise from the Promised Land, a Son of God. Ruth wasn't looking for the blessing or the Man of God. She was looking to the Blesser, the God that kept them. She gained this insight from living within that household. She concurs in chapter 1 verse 16 and solidifies her resolve in verse 17 as she demonstrates that she understands covenant. Ruth 1:16-17 (NKJV), Ruth said, "Entreat me not to leave you, or to turn back from following after you; for wherever you go, I will go; and wherever you lodge, I will lodge; your people shall be my people, and your God, my God. Where you die, I will die, and there will I be buried. The Lord do so to me and more also, if anything but death parts you and me." With this statement Naomi sees Ruth's heart and realizes her tenacity and who she really is. In verse 18, Naomi saw that Ruth was determined to go with her, so she stopped trying to convince her otherwise.

Unfortunately, it sounds like Naomi doesn't realize what treasure she truly has in Ruth upon her return to Israel. Naomi is still stuck in her pity party as she bitterly complains, "I left with my husband and two sons and now I return empty. How do you think that made her daughter-in-law feel? Especially knowing no one would extend their hospitality towards Naomi because she was a foreigner, a cursed moabite. Although, this was said, Ruth still serves wholeheartedly and perhaps all the more.

Naomi returns to a country and a people she knows with such a negative outlook and Ruth arrives to a strange land and people and remains so positive. Ruth has more reason to dread her outcome than Naomi. Instead of moping, Ruth is ready to put her hand to something. You must do something! Nothing just happens even with God orchestrating everything. Ruth went out in faith got up and got going. She did what she knew; she went to work in the field to glean, to survive and believed for favor. She found favor in a divine set-up appointed by God. It turned out where she worked belonged to the suitor God had in mind for Ruth. Therefore, your prince may be right in front of your eyes and you may not even be aware of it...yet. Just keep believing and working towards the goal that is immediately before you, which is your life adventure, your purpose to serve God, not to be confused with the prince. Wait to be noticed! For example, in Ruth 2:5, then Boaz said to his servant who was in charge of the reapers, "Whose young woman is this?"

After being noticed, Ruth was approached and favor was bestowed. Boaz gave Ruth instructions so that he wouldn't lose her to another. She listened and obeyed, showing her submissive heart to the authority over her; therefore, she was given provision and protection. Boaz provided both provision for food for her and Naomi and protection from the men not to touch her per his command. Recognizing his authority and position, that Boaz was not merely a foreman but the top guy she humbly asks, "Why me?" He responds by informing her of all the positive feedback he was told of her. Ladies, your reputation precedes you, your character and integrity will shine through. This is important, as it will be a distinguishing factor that separates women from the girls as it tells the Man of God how you would best represent him and his name.

Furthermore, Boaz' statement to her tells us that he recognizes her as a covenant keeping woman, which is very rare. He sees her heart, obedience, that she is honorable, demonstrates patience, and is hard-working, trustworthy and faithful. Upon paying her this ultimate compliment, he adds a blessing. (Ruth 2:11-12) This blessing restates the one given by Naomi earlier and then is further expounded because now she has journeyed to the promise land and under the wings and protection of God. She may be a foreigner, a gentile, but her conversion is established through her word, deeds and loyalty.

Ruth shows such appreciation and gratitude in being noticed by him. She invites him in her words, "May I continue to find favor in your eyes, my lord." (Ruth 2:13) She compares herself and marvels at his kindness towards her by mentioning how she is poor and lowly compared to the other girls, and yet you still comfort me. From there Boaz invites her to eat with him. Tenderness, appreciation and respect speak to a man. It's these qualities that encouraged Boaz to extend an invitation to her to join him and the others for a meal. This also causes him to want to show her increasingly more favor, as he instructs his workers to purposely leave her more barley than the others and not to embarrass or rebuke her as she works and gleans.

Ruth barely arrived home when Naomi instantly

recognized the favor bestowed on Ruth. Ruth didn't have a chance to tell Naomi anything that had happened on her first day of work. Naomi asked all the questions and Ruth told all she had experienced. What I really liked was what Ruth said in Ruth 2:19…"The name of the man I worked with today is Boaz." Notice she didn't say that she worked for him. Working with him almost makes it sound like they were working side by side, as partners, in a sense they were. Ruth wouldn't have had as much to show for her effort if he hadn't made provision for her. Ruth continued to work in Boaz' fields until the end of the harvest season allowing time for them to learn and know each other.

At the beginning of Ruth chapter 3, it shows the ending of a season and now it's time to move into the next level of progression. Naomi knows the customs, whereas Ruth does not, so Ruth obeys Naomi's instruction by faith and ends up blessed. Naomi tells her to bathe and make herself presentable. Naomi further instructs Ruth to watch and wait, when Boaz is done celebrating the harvest feast notice where he lies down, then go to him and uncover his feet and lie down. How strange to read how Ruth is encouraged to approach the man, when we are taught women are to be found and pursued by the men! Naomi, like any meddling Jewish Mama would do, pushed things along, as she had said earlier that she would find someone to take care of Ruth. She knew she could send Ruth to Boaz in the middle of the night and trust him due to the kindness he had shown Ruth throughout the season.

If Boaz was clueless about Ruth throughout the entire season, he was just as clueless until Ruth spelled it out for him that he was her kinsman redeemer. To further emphasize this she informs him I need you to take care of me by saying…"Spread the corner of your garment over me…" There was no mistaking what she was saying to him. He simply had to respond whether he would accept her or not. Her request touched his heart as we discover that there is a significant age difference. Boaz is much older than Ruth as he addresses her as "daughter" and reiterates this by saying, "…You have not run after the younger men, whether rich or poor." So, this verifies that Ruth saw his character, integrity and that his name was good and not only as the kinsman redeemer. Plus, he was simply "the choice" as no other had been placed before her. She didn't look to the workers she followed, she didn't have her eye on the foreman, but the one man that approached her from the very beginning. As Boaz saw something in Ruth, Ruth too saw something in Boaz. This approach of hers may have been different from the norm; however, it played out the way God intended for this particular love story. Why is that? For whatever reason, even with Boaz' wealth, position, power, good name, he obviously had some insecurity that kept him from pursuing Ruth further. It took Ruth to lay down her pride at his feet to admit she needed him. Now that she laid everything on the line, such as her heart, dignity and reputation, he didn't keep her guessing but equally met her with an immediate response. He had no problem of accepting her to be his wife, to take care of her, accept her liabilities and all that entails being a widow due to her noble character witnessed by all people in the town. So her name was made good out of her respectable conduct that would bring him more honors and would not make his stake for her questionable, either for him or for her. Actually, it would be easy to see how they were brought together. They not only received the blessing of God, their love story writer, but by the townspeople who witnessed all that transpired. With both having notable character, their relationship would be well received as to why these two were coming together although no formal courtship was witnessed. The elders of the town would understand and simply accept that these two knew what kind of commitment they were entering into and be met with the utmost approval and blessing from them all.

Boaz informed Ruth; although, he appreciated her offer he had to be honest that there was another that had more of a right to her as a kinsman redeemer than him so if this man should want her, so be it, this is the rightful "Plan A". However, his heart was into "Plan B", should this man refuse, don't worry as he would step up and receive her. To emphasize his feelings towards her, he promises himself to her in front of God to erase any doubt in her mind or heart. That not being with her wasn't his doing but would be God's. Ruth was going to be redeemed and taken care of one way or the other. However, it would be God's plan for it to happen through Boaz. Ruth couldn't lose, she was in a Win-Win situation as her Father God was looking out for her best interest and now had a good man doing the same. Now they both lied down until morning leaving all they had discussed in God's hands. I wonder how they both slept. In order to keep her and his name and character intact, Boaz instructed her to sleep there until morning, but be the first to get up and leave before anyone wakes. This shows wisdom and care for them both. Boaz is already thinking as a provider and protector. I guess this answers my earlier question; they didn't get much sleep as both of them were up before dawn break as he packed her more food, sent her on her way as he made his way to town.

Once Ruth arrived home and she shared with Naomi all that happened. Ruth was met with this advice from Naomi in Ruth 3:18 (which this chapter is named after, the hardest part of all), "wait, my daughter, until you find out what happens. For the man will not rest until the matter is settled today." This shows the determination of a Man of God. It is truly beautiful when you see a man earnestly strive for what he knows he wants.

What Naomi said was true, while Ruth waited, the Bible says in Ruth 4:1...meanwhile, Boaz went to the town gate and sat there. Therefore, simultaneously as they were talking Boaz was at work. Boaz was such an early bird he had to sit and wait for the elders to arrive to announce his intentions publicly. Boaz had a plan and once the rightful kinsman redeemer arrived he collected him and 10 other elders, to present this plan before them. His presentation, being in right standing within the community, the reputation that Ruth had made for herself, and obviously with God's favor made all the difference. However, do you see how well thought out Boaz' plans were? For getting up so early he certainly was prepared. Look at Ruth 4:5, as he paints the picture for the kinsman redeemer, "Oh, did you realize along with all that land you obtain Ruth and all her property and maintain the name of her late husband." This man quickly gave up the idea of redeeming Ruth and all that went with her, thinking only of him and what he may lose. What compassion this shows of Boaz knowing that he himself would be responsible for these same responsibilities and has no qualms about it. What was simply amazing was to have the rightful kinsman redeemer in Ruth 4:8 state, "Buy it yourself." This further enhances Boaz' integrity showing he wasn't shady about acquiring Ruth and all the property.

He made sure of this by proclaiming to all of what the agreement was and the conditions he was willing to fulfill. Do you notice something about what Boaz just did? He sacrificed himself on the behalf of Ruth. He has nothing to gain but her. Everything that came with her was a loss. The property would cost him, her family's debt, taking care of her mother-in-law, etc. Boaz counted the costs and he found Ruth worthy.

To make his deal sweeter, look at the blessing and what wisdom the town elders spoke to Boaz in Ruth 4:11-12. That is some blessing! That was a God set-up to receive that blessing. God wanted Ruth and Boaz together more than they did or even more than Naomi did. God needed an established Godly lineage and He did so through these two, as God opened Ruth's womb. Here's an interesting thought...Ruth's womb was purposely kept from conceiving from her first husband until Boaz. God is truly a second chance God and has a bigger plan than we truly realize and it was God's will for Ruth to remarry. Not only was her firstborn son a gift to the couple, but to Naomi as she is blessed by the townspeople in Ruth 4:13-14. This firstborn is blessed because the firstborn belongs to God.

Since God knows the end from the beginning; therefore, I believe God really had Ruth's life and love story all planned all along, as God was truly pleased with her. I'm sure Ruth loved her first husband dearly as is clear in her love and respect of Naomi, but through Ruth's servitude, obedience, faithfulness and sacrifice God restored Ruth beyond her wildest imagination with the love of her life and a baby. The bigger picture of their love was they were hand chosen by God to become amazing characters in the Bible and to be in the family line of Perez, which means BREAKTHROUGH and on down to be the great-grand parents of King David and ultimately to the King of Kings our Lord and Savior, Jesus Christ. How amazing is that? So, don't count your love story so short you have no idea what God has in mind for your love story or the significance of whom it is that God brings to you. Don't disregard who he brings based on the outer appearance ask God to see the bigger picture or to see the heart of who he brings. Ruth didn't discard Boaz based on his age or felt she was out of his league due to opposing socioeconomic levels; they simply fell in love based on character, mutual respect, and integrity of oneself and of the other. They met their match, the Godly kind.

What else did you learn from Ruth that is different than what you see in the world today? The loyalty, commitment and love between a mother-in-law and daughter-in-law. Often we hear of the commonplace disrespectful "mother-in-law jokes" and how hurtful this is to family relationships as people accept this as the norm and buy into that garbage. Doing so is so inflicting a wound not only against your prospective mother-in-law but towards your husband as well. I strongly suggest you to get to know this amazing woman God has brought into your life. Recognize how well your husband respects the authority of his mother as it will prove how he will respect and treat you. Not to mention, how well do you want to be treated by future sons / sons-in-law and daughters / daughters-in-law? We reap what we sow.

The Bible shows us the importance of relationships. Through family, Godly wisdom is to be passed down from the more mature women to the younger women. A more mature woman is defined as being more established in her relationship with the Lord not so much as being older in age. For it is these Godly women that truly understand and are much more insightful of God's idea of marriage and the roles of a wife than anything the world would have to offer. The scriptures to support this are Titus 2:3-4.

Knowing I myself have a lot to learn, I simply pray for God to bring me a Godly woman to teach me the ways to love and care for my children better and ultimately prepare me as a wife for the God chosen husband for me. As I wait on God for my answer, I discovered three women that were all in leadership in my church that I kept crossing paths with. I simply narrowed my choices as to who she may be. I asked God to give me wisdom, as I would observe these women further in order to find my "Spiritual Mama". Upon observation the first two were eliminated, leaving the third. I approached her and told her of my prayer and desire to be mentored and if she would pray about it and let me know. We both prayed and came back together. I shared some of my desires in what I was seeking in this type of relationship with both her and her husband. I discovered that we had a difference of opinion in defining the accountability I was seeking in preparation for courtship. Their idea was too lenient for my taste and I wanted a stricter accountability team than offered. Their viewpoint wasn't wrong, it just wasn't right for me. So, I continued to seek the Lord.

Then the day came when God answered my prayer and an awesome Christian brother, who discovered my heart in serving and recognized I had a similar heart that matched his mother's, found me. Knowing that his mother was seeking someone to impart to, he introduced me to her, not knowing my own heart's cry desiring to be imparted to by such a Godly woman. I'll never forget the day that my spiritual mama entered into my life. I'll never forget her beautiful face. During that moment, I thought to myself, "Why does she look so familiar to me?" Although, I knew we had never met before. We met at church after the 11:00 am Sunday morning service on October 23, 2005 and then spoke again after the evening service. I told her, "I want what you have. You are seeing the legacy of your children serving God now, not just hoping that they will after you die. I'm looking for a Spiritual Mother to impart to me." In loving response and surprise she said, "I believed God for someone to impart to." Ironically, her son and my Christian brother didn't know these words were exchanged as he departed right before the evening service for a plane trip, all he had said briefly to her before saying goodbye was, "Mom, get to know Daphne. She is a good friend to have." To this day both she and I are ever so grateful to him for keeping his spiritual eyes open and introducing us to each other.

Doesn't this just make you want to have a Spiritual Mama of your own? That's what the Story of Ruth and that verse in Titus did for me. Now if you want a Spiritual Mama, you need to have an idea of what qualities you would like for her to have. List what areas you need support and instruction in. Begin to pray for God to bring her into your life. What do you do once you have someone in mind? After prayer, careful observation, approach them about the idea and pray some more. Once agreed, establish your commitment and watch what God does in both of your lives. You both will be richer for it, trust me. As far as establishing a commitment, my spiritual mama and I have committed to meet weekly to share the Word of God together, pray over each other's children, share life stories and experiences with one another and do fun girly outings together. I highly respect, admire and appreciate her heart, wisdom and input. I simply thank God for the season He gave me a spiritual mama.

Another suggestion may be to check with your church for a mentoring group of women. Perhaps instead of having just one very insightful mature Godly woman, there are a few Godly women that could offer you a lot more wealth of knowledge to impart into you. If not, see if your church or women's ministry would want to start a group to not only bless you, but be a blessing to other ladies seeking Godly mentors.

Whether you have a Spiritual Mother, want one or not, please still follow this suggestion. Begin to pray in advance for who your mother-in-law will be. You will want to have a good, healthy and solid relationship with your mother-in-law. This will not only bless you, but bless her and her son which will be/is your husband. I was given this great advice by a friend who I had witness how God brought an amazing Man of God into her life. However, her relationship with her mother-in-law is a hurtful one for her. She said to me, "Daphne, had I only known or even thought to pray for her while I prayed for the Man of God." Knowing my friend's heart, I know she would want me to pass on this wisdom to you. Pray for your mother-in-law now! I am grateful for her insight.

I am grateful God answered my prayer to send me my spiritual mother. Then I have no doubt that He will answer my prayer for a beautiful relationship with my future mother-in-law. Therefore, both my friend and my spiritual mother would have prepared me to be ready to establish an amazing relationship with my future mother-in-law. Remember you not only marry the Man of God but you marry his family right along with him and vice-versa. So pray for his relationship with your family, too.

Homework:

1. Was this your first time reading the book of Ruth? Had you read Ruth before? Under what circumstances led you to read Ruth?

2. Did this chapter offer you more insight since reading Ruth?

3. Share from your notes what you took as you originally read Ruth.

4. Make a list of traits for a Spiritual Mother and pray for one.

5. Observe Godly mature women to be a possible mentor.

6. If you already have one, please share the benefits you have received since having this incredible woman in your life.

7. Begin praying for your mother-in-law. What are some things you would like to do with her? How could your relationship with your mother-in-law be a blessing to your husband and ultimately your own marriage?

8. What other relationships do you need to pray for in advance?
   Such as on either side yours or his, for the Fathers-in-law, children of a previous relationship, brothers and sister, etc.?

Chapter 9

The Life Changing Revelation

As much as you want your Man of God to enter into your life or you think you're ready for the relationship, you really are not. At least not until you have your life changing revelation but that doesn't happen until you are willing to let God deal with you, your heart and your pain. It has taken time to build up your defenses, your walls or modes of self-preservation, so simply accept the fact that it will take time to break them down.

How do you do this? First, come to the realization that you must go through the restoration process, no more avoiding it, withdrawing or running from it. The sooner you face it and embrace it the better. Depending on the severity of the pain and the duration of harboring it may determine the length of the recovery process. Your honesty with yourself and God in uncovering it and dealing with it sets the pace of your healing. Restoration is healthy, but it is painful; however, it's worth it! If you endured the blows, the hurt, the pain, that caused wounds and scars of your broken heart, and held onto strongholds in your mind, while it caused pain upon receipt. Therefore, it will cause pain in its elimination. There are no shortcuts. Trust me, you wouldn't want it any other way, it would only prolong the healing process. Why would you want to do that? Haven't you had enough? No more being comfortable with the pain. Let's deal with it!

You may ask, "How do I deal with it?" Prayer...it truly changes things. Not so much does the prayer change the situation as your prayer changes you as it comes from your heart. That's why it's best to come up with a heartfelt prayer of your own, but here's one to get you started in case you simply find yourself at a complete loss for words.

Pray the following:

Heavenly Father, I come before you now asking for your help because I can't fix or deal with this pain in my heart on my own, but you can. Please heal me from the very depths of my heart and all it contains inside and out, until I am fully healed, whole and restored. I know and expect my restoration to be painful, so please be gentle. Thank you for binding the broken hearted and for loving me through the process. I know I can trust you through this. Thank you for loving me so much that you refuse to allow me to carry this hurt any longer. Give me the strength and courage to confront the pain and be rid of it. Please bring divine friendships into my life. Friends that have already experienced successful restoration to encourage me as well as those growing through it so I don't feel alone in my own journey. Thank you for hearing my prayer. I know I have prayed according to your will, so I believe that I have received all that I have asked, in Jesus' name, Amen.

One sure way of recognizing the depth of your pain is if you avoid being alone. You constantly need to keep busy, and distracted from thinking about it, dealing with it, and want to avoid feeling lonely. You don't want to cry yet again. By day, you surround yourself with superficial relationships. You're nice to people and get along well with others but you keep people at a distance and they feel they know you, but you know better. If you must be home alone, (and the nights are the worst), you create a lot of noise, with music, or phone calls just to keep your mind preoccupied from your thoughts. God is there waiting to begin the process, so your avoidance isn't from the hurt you experienced, you are avoiding God, knowing He is saying to you, "It's time to deal with this."

Not knowing your background, experiences, personality or loss and I don't know your perception of God. However, if you've been in a relationship with Him for a while and have begun to really trust Him, then this process will be much easier. Whereas a person who is embarking on a new relationship with God needs to establish trusting Him before this can be done. Please keep this in mind, just as you wouldn't share all your painful experiences right away with a newly made friend, it simply would take time to uncover these deep places of the heart with them as it may with God. Therefore, be patient with yourself.

God is the ultimate gentleman. Remember, He already knows you better than you know yourself. He knows how much you hurt. He knows what hurts you and who caused it. He will be gentle with you. No matter what he asks you to do remember it's for your good, it's to help you and it will heal you. Whatever you do, don't stop doing what God tells you to do regardless of the pain, keep pushing through it. Don't Quit!

You may wonder, what will He tell me to do? You need to continue to journal, express your feelings in order to be honest with yourself and with Him. Pray and work on becoming the person you are meant to be and be open. You should be journaling throughout every chapter of this book it will bring healing. Praying is powerful, this displays humility as you admit you don't know what to do or how to do anything and so you give it to God and allow Him to lead you where to go, what to say, what to do and how to say it or how to do whatever it is He tells you. As you become the person you're meant to be by developing those traits listed in chapter 7, you will discover what it is you are meant to be doing. Don't worry you won't be thrown into doing something too overwhelming. God will ease you into it a little at a time. Although, He will have you leave your comfort zone to venture out at each phase to produce growth. You might think it's too much, but God will not give you more than you can handle or conquer ever!

As part of your growth, He will bring people into your life to assist in the process. More than likely you will not realize that is what He has in mind as new friends appear. Before you know it, these new friends become closer to you than you had planned to let in. You didn't even notice when your first "outer wall" cracked and came down. After spending more time with your friends, you learn more about them and they learn more about you, you begin to wonder since when did they get this close to you? You may become uncomfortable with this "closeness" or with them knowing so much of your experiences/background. Whether you know it or not you may consider "sabotaging" the friendship. Sabotage by doing any of the following; 1) withdrawing from them all of a sudden, 2) being irritable, but blaming it on them, 3) blowing a disagreement out of proportion, 4) faultfinding to give you reasons why you should stop being their friend, etc. The only way you get over that is to stick with them through these uncomfortable feelings. You don't have to necessarily tell them what you're going through or feeling. In fact, I discovered that it's best that you don't, just let them "love" you as friends through it. This keeps them behaving naturally.

Once you admit to yourself that you have allowed a friend or two into your world and a friendship has begun and is being maintained, safety is usually offered. If not, don't hesitate to ask, "Are we safe enough with each other to talk about our friendship?" Reassurance needs to be offered. For instance, explain your definition of friendship so no one is set up for failure to not meet the expectation of the other. Allow for one another to be real honest and can have safe, not hurtful or overly critical talk. If necessary, explain how you are as a person, to prevent misunderstandings concerning your responses or theirs to you. After successfully opening up to 1-2 people, it won't be long before God will send others. What for? Some are sent to keep you social and others to become long-term friends.

After you feel comfortable freely sharing, discussing, asking different things and you have a history of friendship established between you for a while the honesty can be reached more easily in progressive degrees.

Another part of my restoration was getting rid of material items from my past, as a form of "letting go". I was at a women's conference when I was challenged to ask God what I was hoarding that I needed to be rid of. He told me what to give away otherwise it would bring a curse into my future. For other women that I've talked to I learned they have done the same thing. Some princesses believing for a Godly remarriage; this meant giving up their old wedding dresses, wedding rings, gifts, furniture, etc. as a way to prevent bringing a reminder of their past into their new future.

Homework: Read 1 Peter 5:10

1. Do you have any friends? Have you met any new friends? What are you doing to meet some?

2. The friends you have, how close are you to them?

3. If you didn't have any friends before, have you discovered some through your group study? If so, please share the difference made in your life since meeting regularly.

4. Did you go through any of the "sabotage" steps? If not any of those listed, what did you experience as you were becoming familiar with having an intimate friend in your life?

5. Keep writing in your journal. Do you recognize any progress or growth?

6. Do you have anything you need to be rid of from a former relationship in order for you to start off fresh with your chosen prince? This could be emotional baggage or actual material possessions? (Such as, love letters, stuffed animals, etc.)

   Wives: If you didn't know to do this before getting married, ask God is there anything you're keeping that you need to get rid of so that He can work on your marriage. Is there anything you've discovered your husband has kept and it hinders your relationship? Then pray and ask God to deal with your husband about this. Write it in your journal and update it as progress is made.

7. To keep your relationships healthy keep the people factor in the back of your mind when dealing with others. I learned this from my church's women's Bible study.

VEP – Very Enjoyable People are those that you enjoy their company, conversations, outings and generally make you feel good about yourself.

VIP – Very Important People are those people that challenge you by telling you the truth and cause you to grow personally.

VDP – Very Dangerous People are those people that drain you emotionally, time stealers, etc. These are people you need to avoid. Only spiritually mature Christians can handle these type people, if they choose to.

Do you have people that fit any of these categories? Which ones do you have more of? What changes do you need to make to surround yourself with more VEPs and VIPs? Which of these are you? What changes do you need to make to be a VEP or VIP to others?

.

WHEN YOU'RE READY FOR THE FAIRYTALE

Chapter 10

Fear No More

Fear is the biggest lie to prevent you from meeting your prince. Fear isn't even original. It will throw the same old lies at us all. Why? These lies have worked so well in the past against so many princesses. But not us! We need to get equipped and take authority and shout, "Fear No More are you going to hinder me!" To equip you, let's discuss the most commonly used deceptive lies. Awareness is important, but the Truth shall make you free! There are so many lies that penetrate our mind, here's some that frequently come up that I myself have combated as well as those women I have spoken with. Do any of these lies sound familiar to you?

Lie # 1 – I'm not worth it! I don't deserve a Mighty Man of God. I'm too much trouble. I'm too much for him to handle.

Truth – You are so worth it! Jesus thought so, He died for you! You have been listening too long to the lies that now you have bought into it. Establish your relationship with Jesus and find out who you are and whose you are and you will find your worth in Him. Not only do you deserve a Mighty Man of God, he will be the only kind of man you will want. There is nothing more beautiful than to see a man sold out for God. If you feel like you are too much trouble or too much to handle, these are probably lies you've believed since childhood. The oldest lies are the hardest to stop believing. Find out where these lies originated and confront them.

Lie # 2 – This relationship is going to end up like the others. Why bother letting him in my heart he's only going to break my heart and/or leave me like all the males in my life!

Truth - No, this relationship will not end up like your past relationships because you included God in it this time. Plus, remember you are not the same person. You have changed on this journey and are still evolving; especially, if you allowed God to select your husband. You put God first before the MOG or yourself. Remember a true MOG will love you more than himself. He will want to protect, provide, and will cherish you. These statements are from a person that needs to experience healing and learn to trust again. Let God help you and when He brings the right MOG into your life, God will use him to aid in your healing.

Lie # 3 - I have nothing to offer him.

Truth – Don't sell yourself short. You are so special and have a unique gift, and that gift is your heart. There is no one else like you. There is a prince just for you that needs the treasure of a heart that only you have to give. You would be surprised at all that is in you and what you truly have to offer.

Lie # 4 – The Mighty Man of God is too good for me.

Truth – Believe it or not the MOG struggles with this about you. When he sees your heart, he will ask God, "Do I deserve such a gift as her?" God chose each of you for the other, simply trust Him, He knows what He's doing. He's been God for a long time.

Lie # 5 – He's a Mighty Man of God, but he's not where I'm at spiritually.

Truth – This is a real misconception that can be deceiving. I don't believe that a couple is ever at the same level in their relationship with the Lord at the same time. If we are to be strong while the other is weak that includes this area, too. The other will encourage the other to strive for a deeper, richer and more meaningful relationship with the Lord. At the same time, I don't think it's wise for a mature Christian to be yoked with a brand new baby Christian. It is known that most women are the spiritual leaders than most men. Women truly want the MOG to be the spiritual leader and to challenge them to a higher level of relating with God; this is still possible even if at the beginning she is more spiritually established than her MOG. It takes love, patience and humility to step back and allow the MOG to grow into his leadership position, but it will be worth it! God will honor this and grow him up quick and it will be the princess striving to catch up to her MOG. I've seen it happen.

Lie # 6 – God can forgive me for my past, but I don't think he can.

Truth – Of course, he can; otherwise, he's not your MOG or not ready to be a MOG. To be A Man of God means he's a Christian so he had to come to the Lord the same way you did, to ask for forgiveness of his sin and past. We are to forgive one another as Christ has forgiven us. If the MOG can't forgive you, then he has some growing still left to do or move on.

Lie # 7 – The Mighty Man of God is only marrying me out of obedience or charity not out of love, want or desire.

Truth – Every love story that God puts together will be different. Those that have more of an arranged marriage may tend to feel like this, but God reassures that this is not the case. A strong MOG will not be coerced, manipulated or forced into a relationship or marriage. A MOG with true integrity doesn't say or do anything that he doesn't mean. So, if he proposes, it's from his heart with sincere love and desire and not out of sheer obedience.

Lie # 8 – Since I allowed God to choose my husband, God chose someone for me that I would never have picked. I'm not even attracted to this person. How is there going to be any romance?

Truth – The beauty of this is that God knows what's best for you, even better than you know for yourself so you have to trust Him in this area just like you would any other. I understand this is harder because it's more personal, but the same principle does apply. The love, romance and even attraction will grow, it may come a little later but it will come. You may even notice yourself developing a different sense of attraction for your MOG. The Bible says true attraction is based on falling in love with the person's heart, character, integrity and his name. His name? Yeah, you should be proud to take on the name of your MOG for who he is and what he represents. You will be representing him as well. Like with all of us, we all have something beautiful in us, simply look deeper for it, it's there and you will be delighted in the gift of the MOG, God has brought only to you. He's entrusted you with this MOG, and with his heart and dreams. Simply enjoy discovering why God chose you to better enhance him.

Lie # 9 – The Mighty Man of God needs help. Changes are necessary in order for this to work. I just can't see how this would even be possible.

Truth – Maybe there are some areas that need improvement, but you are no different. God is not done working and improving on either of you yet. This is a very judgmental, selfish and critical stance; maybe you're not ready if this is how you feel. Remember you are not to enter a relationship wanting or expecting to change a person only God can do that. When God changes a person then you know the change is permanent. You are only called to love and accept the person whether they change or not. If you can't live with or accept the person as is, then move on. Just be sure you are not being too critical. The person God has for you will be the right person, not the perfect person.

Lie # 10 – I can't keep a Mighty Man of God happy.

Truth – First of all, it is not your responsibility to make the MOG happy, he must do that for himself. You are to simply come alongside him to enjoy life with him, as you love him, care for him and encourage him. If you seek the Lord to be the wife that God wants you to be and you pray to be the wife your MOG needs, how could you go wrong? Ask your MOG what he expects and needs of you and do your best, no one can ask for more. God created your MOG for you and you for your MOG so you have it in you to create a happy home.

Remember God hasn't given you a spirit of fear, but of power, love and a sound mind. (2 Tim 1:7) For you have the mind of Christ, as long as you belong to Him. You are a warrior princess with full armor use it! Cast down any evil imagination that exalts itself above God, that means anything that is contrary to what God says about you and He says you are His daughter. Last time I checked, it's the prince that needs to measure up to the standard of a princess. Not that we princesses are better than the princes, but us women are to offer to the men someone worth fighting for. If we don't hold ourselves to a higher standard then how can we expect such from them? God will not have you unequally yoked. We are promised and betrothed to "one" and that one is a predetermined, predestined prince specifically chosen by God, if we allow Him and if we agree not to meddle or settle for less than His best.

These are just some of the lies that may surface during your healing process. Don't believe the lies, but recognize that they are proof of your progress in your preparation. Depending on your pace of healing you will become stronger in ridding your mind of such falsehoods. The best thing you can do is to develop a closer, deeper and more intimate relationship with God to increase your strength against these negative thoughts and images that may flood your mind. For example, if the thought enters your mind that you will make the same mistakes as you did in the past. Remember that's not true because you are no longer that person. Not convinced? You have decided to take this journey by committing to God and yourself to be celibate while you heal from your past issues. You are journaling, praying, having a Bible Study, you have a support group (if conducting a group study), you're making new friends and doing the homework at the end of each chapter (I hope). This is a big difference! If you want change you have to do something different and you have.

Imagine these lies, negative thoughts and images are trying to hold you back, trap you as if you are the princess locked in the tower. It's not up to the prince to rescue and free you; he's not even in the picture yet. You don't want to be the damsel in distress, be the warring princess that you are. You are stronger than you think and if you're not, you need to be. Your husband will only be as strong as the support that is backing him up, that means you. You've been reading the Bible along with this book, get more familiar with it. We need to know it contains kingdom promises to help us princesses speak life and blessings over our princes to keep them strengthened, encouraged and protected as they fight for us. Before you can apply these crucial scriptures on the MOG's behalf, you must learn how to use them for yourself. Remember negative thoughts, images, comments will continually pop in your mind or be said to you to get you to stop believing for a healthy, godly relationship. Fear is an ongoing battle and the first lie you deal with will be the hardest. It's usually a stronghold in your mind that is difficult to dismiss, keep working at it, it will eventually give and be broken and never to be believed again. After that first one, it will get easier for you to recognize other lies needing to be purged.

The best way to be rid of fear is to use faith. Faith cannot operate where fear is present. It's your faith that causes your fairytale to come true. How bad do you want your fairytale? When you get to the point that you are so driven to see and believe for it to happen, then your faith will increase and grow stronger. Then your fairytale will grow closer to being manifested in your life. How encouraging is that?

Another thing, do not let others discourage you or your faith simply because they do not understand your commitment to waiting on God for your fairytale or for the prince. There are people in your life that love you, want to protect you, want to help you and definitely want you happy and married off. Keep this in mind when they start budding into your personal life by offering suggestions to get you dating. You may be told to go online to meet someone, or to clubs, or parties, etc. God knows where you are and is responsible for divine appointments to happen regularly. Like with everything, simply ask Him. It could be what God uses to bring the prince to you, wait on His green light. Instead of those places why not wait to be found while serving in church or in ministry? That's where Men of God congregate. Don't let anyone push you and don't let impatience move you ahead of God's timing. Part of the fairytale is how it perfectly works out so don't sell yourself short by rushing, simply focus on God, then you can't go wrong. The closer you are to God the closer you are to meeting the prince, your Man of God.

Homework:

1. List all your fears in your journal. Then list possible solutions how to overcome those fears.

   Wives: Lies, fear and doubt didn't stop thwarting your thoughts when you got married. What lies, fears or doubts come to mind to second guess your commitment to your marriage?

2. What Bible scriptures help you in fighting those negative thoughts, images and fears? Write them out and read them often.

3. Write down what possible things other people would suggest for you to do to meet someone. Jot down your refusal to such ideas if you're not interested in taking them up on their suggestions.

   Wives: If you experience a tough time in your marriage write down what others say for you to do to "solve" your marital problems. Then write down your rebuttal/argument against accepting their "solutions" so you don't give consideration to their words.

4. What lie mentioned in the reading could you relate to? What lies do you believe that weren't listed? (If you need support or encouragement to combat any of these lies share with your group or a close friend.)

DAPHNE M. HUNTER

Chapter 11

Recognizing Your Value

What is amazing about our God, our Father, the King is that He places such value on His girls, His daughters, you and me. This is nothing new for Him, as it is very clear in His Word, even during a time and place where females were not regarded or esteemed. In the Old Testament, God the Father announced His daughters have rights as the men do. In the New Testament, Jesus challenged the culture of the treatment of women. We are loved, accepted and adored by our God and King. Allow me to show you in His Word that you are highly regarded and not to forget how valued you truly are.

Let's begin in the Old Testament. In Genesis we are a gift to man and to the world as we bring life and told along with man to have dominion. We are an asset. Our presence brings beauty, is a blessing and will benefit and bring great bounty to our men, the world and our Creator. After man fell into sin then the original order of dominion changed into domination. Since then, we, women are to come under the covering and headship of the men. God re-established a new order due to our sin, so if He said it, we are to accept it.

However, with fallen men as our covering, the headship role is sometimes likely to be misinterpreted and/or abused. If this is the case, perhaps they feel their role is justified and explains why men sometimes no longer see us as their equal, or their counterpart, but as the problem and the blame. Therefore, we have lost rights in their eyes and are to be controlled and dominated without a voice. Until we see 5 unified sisters rise up, stand up and challenge a wrong against them. They collectively said, "We accept our place, our role, our position, our authorities over us, but No More to being stripped of what is rightfully ours." We see change in the perception of how these women, also daughters of God, finally saw themselves in their own eyes. Then we see their strength as they came together and challenged the status quo.

You can find these sisters in Numbers 27:1-7. The scripture begins with who they are and where they came from, they were known by who their father was and the generations before them. Same as you are known by who your Father is and are called by your name. These women knew who they were individually and collectively. It was when they were in unity they recognized their strength, power and value. Therefore, they could approach with boldness before all and state their cause, to fight for their rightful inheritance and the promise given to them. They were not about to allow anyone or anything to steal their hope, faith or promise from them. Notice what happens next. In Numbers 27:5; Moses brought their case before the Lord. Moses was the head authority and wise, this tells me that Moses recognized the validity of their case that even he had to go to God to give a just answer.

Not only did God, the Father, YOUR FATHER, grant these women what was rightfully theirs, but had Moses set a precedent for all future generations, including OURS, to establish our promised inheritances, dreams and visions. Our Father defended our sisters of the past and is defending us now. He validated us, our rights to what is promised to us as princesses. If we were of no value there would be no need for validation. Then Moses wouldn't have bothered approaching God. See? Those men didn't know the value of women, but when God set them straight only then did they see. So, why are we looking to men to validate us when only God can?

Regardless of what dream or promise God has given you, including the promised prince, your Mighty Man of God, and it doesn't appear to be materializing don't settle and accept that. Fight! Challenge what it looks like in the natural until it changes. Refuse to be apathetic that it won't happen, refuse to be wronged, refuse to be denied and refuse to be discriminated when you know what God has told and shown you! He will validate you, your dream, your vision and you will be granted your promise. Don't accept anything less than God's best for you because you're worth it. Face it girl, you're valuable!

Then there are those of you rehearsing your past after reading that last line. Don't you think God knows your past? Yet He still feels and says the same thing, "YOU ARE WORTHY! YOU ARE VALUABLE!!" Look at Jesus, the ultimate gift. He restores 3 women with a past that any gossipmonger would love to get a hold of. There's the woman to be stoned, the woman who washed His feet with her tears and dried them with her hair and the Samaritan woman who had 5 husbands and currently living with another man. Did this embarrass Jesus? Did this stop Him from talking to them? Did this prevent Him from making Himself known to them or stop Him from forgiving them? NO! In fact, He used them in spite of their backgrounds to spread His gospel. The Samaritan woman was responsible for leading an entire city to Him.

Jesus saw her value before He even died for her. He sees that value and then some in you, and that's why He died for you. Now you've got to see it in yourself!

If you don't know already, you need to know how truly precious you are to your Father, the King. Once you accept this fact, you will experience healing and you will begin to walk, talk and conduct yourself in confidence. Not a confidence in oneself but in response to the love realized. This confidence is further heightened after being found and pursued by the Man of God. There is nothing that looks more beautiful on a woman than when she is all aglow as a result from being loved. Not just "in love" but having been "found, pursued and loved".

First, a woman must be found. I don't believe a woman can be found until she is knowledgeable of who she is in Christ. After understanding the authority bestowed to her then she is able to walk in it. Accepting this authority is the start to her confidence level being boosted. As she adjusts to her new, found confidence and embraces it, then she exudes confidence constantly and this is what catches the attention of those around her including the prospective Man of God.

Catching his eye is not considered "being found". Let's establish a definition of what "being found" means. In this case, being found will be defined as having drawn the attention of a man to the point of curiosity, that you are approached, invited into a setting to become more personable and may later on include meeting significant people in his life. The purpose of him having you meet key people in his life is to welcome feedback concerning the prospect of you joining him at various functions in the future and this shows wisdom. This man may at first see your personality but once he sees your character and your heart, the core of who you are and he states his intentions to enter courtship, then you have been found. The Bible says in Proverbs 18:22, "Who ever finds a wife, finds a good thing and obtains favor of the Lord", (NKJV) in the Message Bible it says, "Find a good spouse, you find a good life and even more; the favor of God." Since you are waiting for the "one" Man of God in particular, being found by another doesn't count. Don't worry you will know the difference when you have been "found by the one" and when you're "noticed by the others". If in doubt, God will reveal it to you.

After enduring the peaks and the valleys of life, it is inevitable for the question to come to mind, how much longer before I share this road with someone? You are given no answer, just keep moving, going on, and living alone. Until you are no longer distracted by this question and your bout with loneliness has once again subsided and you keep doing what you know what to do. In the least unexpected times you are "found". I was "found" and found myself clueless. It took some time for me to get it and then even longer to really get it. How did I really get it? God had to tell me. You would think why did God have to tell you? There are several answers that it could be. It could be that even with my walls basically down, my past hurt still blinded me, or with my personality I am naturally outgoing and friendly, so I don't read into anything when a man approaches me, and since it has been a long time being in the company of a man I didn't catch the innuendos or recognize that he was flirting with me. With all of that in mind this can make it very easy not to recognize once you've been found. This is all true; however, what really caught me by surprise was to discover that I had been "found" not according to what I would call being found.

God set me up. I was "found" initially by a Man of God, and then God had me meet the other significant people in his life casually unaware to me or him. Trust me God has a plan and He will execute it one way or another. Don't worry as you struggle with waiting to be found, you're not lost (smile), you're not forgotten, God knows where you are and He knows where the prince is. According to God's timing, you will be "found" by the Man of God whether he knows he's found you or not. As time progressed, God told me, "You've been found." I knew that wasn't just by anyone, but the one. God is no respecter of persons, if he told me, he will tell you once the time comes.

So, you've been found, now what? Get familiar with that question, especially if your Man of God is shy or slow in his approaching you, he may not even realize what he's "found" yet. Be patient. The next part after being found is being pursued. Like being found may not be based on your idea of what you have in mind, you can totally miss being pursued, too. I certainly hope not, because being pursued is the fun part for us girls. To most of us, we assume being pursued is when we are asked on a date repeatedly and that definitely is true, because that's the physical representation of the pursuit, but it's not the only method. Try imagining being mentally pursued or spiritually. All three of these areas are closely tied into the emotional jumpstart of something as you are pursued in any of these areas. The connection between you and your pursuing prince will either set aflame or fizzle out. Should the connection be there, the fiery pursuit will continue.

The mental pursuit is a pursuit of conversation, lots of questions as you learn how each other thinks and feels about things. You may experience more "phone dates" then actual outings, which is fine for a while, but can be seen as discouraging if not balanced with a change of surroundings from time to time. Another way to alleviate any discouragement is the number of times being called, texts received, type of messages left, or the willingness of the prince to be accommodating to fit the needs and/or schedule of the princess.

The spiritual pursuit is very interesting and quite intense. The world is more familiar with the physical pursuit. In fact, "too familiar" and familiar with mentally stimulating conversation and leaves it at that. The spiritual pursuit goes right to the heart of a person; this is the most personal facet of a person. Rightfully so, since your relationship with the Lord and Savior, Jesus Christ should be of an extreme personal nature. In this pursuit and through the most informative talks, here is the meat, as you begin to find out if you will or will not be unequally yoked. This is a serious discovery that needs to be dealt with before the heart gets involved. Back tracking after the heart has been shared could be painful. As you seek to discover what common interests you have in general, the same goes for your relationship with God. How do you both view God? What doctrinal beliefs does each of you hold to? How regularly do you go to church? What ministries are you involved in and how involved are you? Later you can discuss what expectations you hold for the husband and wife roles after considering what the Bible says.

After the pursuit, the next step is courtship. The

world calls it dating.   Dating is completely different with God involved, so I call it courtship. You would never hear anyone from the world use that word.

After being pursued this allows your heart to be revealed, enough to allow the prince to determine to continue further down the road to see if you are his princess or not. Regardless, boundaries need to be established in order to guard your hearts from being too vulnerable. Sharing your thoughts, feelings, beliefs and other things, ultimately your heart, is just as intimate as sex if not more so, if you're not careful you could be setting yourself up for failure. The best way to measure this is to ask yourself these questions (#3-5) in order to keep yourself true to your Man of God. These questions show you already are beginning or do have love, care and respect for your one and only

Homework:

1. Do you feel valuable? If not, did this chapter help you see how God sees you as valuable?

2. How do you see yourself? Before and then after reading this chapter.

    How would my prince/husband feel about...?

3. The topic I'm discussing with this other prince?

4. The duration or time of night that I am talking to another princess' prince/husband?

5. Would I want my prince/husband doing the same with another princess?

6. Read about Jacob and his wives Leah and Rachel in Genesis 29.

   This chapter is very interesting as it adds to a fascinating discussion concerning both this chapter and prepares you for the next. Knowing how hard Jacob worked for Rachel, do you think she would be considered valuable? In having to work harder and longer for Rachel, do you think this cause Jacob to make some personal changes to himself in order to prepare for the wife, he loved?

DAPHNE M. HUNTER

Chapter 12

The Decoy

As you know, we women have to be extremely careful with our hearts. "For where your treasure is, there your heart will be also." (Matthew 6:21) That's why we must treasure the King more than anything else. If our heart is set on Him then no one can touch our heart or damage it, we have given it to Him for safekeeping.

In the world we are clueless of the Great Love our King has for us so we are use to having to kiss a lot of frogs before hopefully finding the prince. Since we don't have to do that and choose not to, then we might think we are out of the woods of being misled. That is so not the case.

Our enemy has studied us well, and knows what we like and don't like.

He sends imposter after imposter as we wait on our prince. So, how can we protect our heart and fight off the temptation of falling for an imposter? Your first line of defense is your journal. Hope you ladies have been writing in them and doing your homework. There was a reason for it and it's for your own good. Remember your assignment from chapter 3 the characteristics of your ideal Man of God. If the imposter doesn't line up with your list, then shrugging him off is no big deal and your heart is saved. Then the imposter of all imposters arrives. He actually matches a lot of what you have asked God for, but not everything. So, what makes this the wrong guy? Something about him will detour you from your relationship with God; although, everything else looks real good. Do NOT Justify it by thinking, "So, what is that one little area compared to all of his other qualities?   Be Strong!

If the enemy sends an imposter, then what is the decoy? The decoy is a Christian brother that is very much alike, if not completely qualified to be your Man of God. His purpose is to prepare you for your actual prince, husband-to-be. Why would we need a decoy? The decoy is going to be a very good friend to you in the long run, whether you or he knows it or not. For example, you cannot jump from an imposter immediately to your Man of God.   You need to learn, adjust and master a few changes in the transition so that when the Man of God enters your life you are not just prepared; you are ready for this God ordained relationship. Be very careful, as it is very easy to fall for the wrong prince. Listen well to God's leading as He speaks to you of things to look for only in your prince. This will help in guarding your heart from any unnecessary heartbreak.

Where in the Bible do we see a man preparing a princess, a future bride for her husband-to be?   You already read Esther. Remember the eunuch, Hegai; see Esther 2:8-9. Due to having such favor with Hegai, Esther received special privileges not obtained by the other prospective brides. Who won the king's heart and the throne? Need I say anything more? Your Father God, the King wants you to have those same special privileges over your Man of God's heart, like no other woman could ever have, that's why you both are specifically made for each other. God wants to prepare you so He sends you a decoy like Hegai. Your Christian brother may or may not know that he is part of your preparation for your husband-to-be. You don't have to necessarily disclose this to him, it's up to you, but I highly suggest you pray about this first.

How does a decoy prepare you? It depends on where you are at spiritually, mentally, emotionally and socially. Not knowing what your personal experiences has been, or the kind of relationship you have with Jesus, what boundaries you have set for yourself, how open you are to others, etc. makes it difficult to answer this question. I will use myself for example. I set standards for myself that are right for me and the situation I live in. However, I have been told that compared to others, my standards are a bit extreme. Although, I mostly stick to my high standards, they have been occasionally tweaked for given situations. There's a lot to learn during the preparation period. Such as, I have learned and still learning what topics are appropriate for discussion, how to present myself, know when to be bold, when to be quiet, how to argue in a healthy manner, learn how to just "be", to be more open when talking, willing to listen and learn another person, becoming more accommodating to the other person, etc. This will aid you in a smoother transition to being the right woman for the Man of God.

Personally, I have learned we, women cannot create a list of desirable traits for the prince that we, princesses are not willing to demand of ourselves. You can't expect him to do all the changing to add up to your desired list. Also, don't plan on changing him after you say "I do". Consider this, as you are being prepared by the decoy, you may discover there are more changes needing to be made in you than you originally thought. God will reveal to you what these changes are. They may not be easy, but you will notice you are more willing to make the effort then ever before. God has a gentle way of wooing you to be willing. It is so convincing that you begin on them right away. Your attitude towards your changing will determine how important is coming alongside your future husband is to you. If you arrive at the point there is nothing you won't do for him, you are on your way. I would like to believe simultaneously God is preparing and encouraging him to make the reasonable changes to be the Man of God you desire. God is a God of mutual blessing and He knows all too well the desires of all of our hearts. Both our hearts and the hearts of our princes are equally important to Him and to serving His kingdom.

So, what areas do you want to improve yourself? Is God dealing with you in any of these or other areas? Below is a list of possible suggestions to help improve yourself as you make yourself ready for the prince. These were the most common categories brought up by women I talked with.

Spiritually – Develop a strong prayer life in general. Pray daily for your MOG. ("If you want to be a wife you must start acting like one by praying for him now. Don't wait until you get married, start praying for him now! It may be your prayers that lead him to you.") My favorite is to pray the "armor of God" over my MOG found in Ephesians 6:10-20. We must prepare them for battle before leaving the home by covering them with prayer, so polish their armor, pray for their strength and endurance. Pray for their specific needs. Upon their return home, wash them with the Word as they find refuge in your arms. Pray for your armor, keep journaling, perhaps create a prayer journal, read the Bible, pray and fast.

Physically – Pay attention to your diet, exercise and any supplements you are or plan on taking. (See 1Timothy 4:8) Being physically prepared is profitable; as you wouldn't want to be disqualified from doing all God would have you do for His kingdom.

Emotionally – Allow God to heal you in the secret places, make new friends, rediscover old friends, journal regularly (one for MOG and one for you personally) and have fun with hobbies or activities that make you relax.

Mentally – Keep the Word of God before you and learn and memorize verses, read books, listen to (praise & worship) music, etc.

Socially – Ask God what activities to participate in, decline, resign from, what people to mentor, what people to glean from, what people to minimize spending time with, which people to avoid that are too emotionally draining, etc.

Remember, it is possible that not all will experience a decoy in their life; however, the majority of people that I have asked that have successful Christian marriages do recall having a practice person before the legitimate prince showed up. One saying that I have heard over and over again from those happily married princesses was, "Your Man of God is never the one you think it is it's the one that comes afterwards."

An excellent question that I have been asked is this, "If I told God that I don't want to date at all, I just want Him to send the MOG, will He still send me a decoy first?" Truthfully, only God knows for each individual situation. As for my personal experience, I told God the exact same thing. "God I don't want to go down that road again. I'm tired of the games and don't want my time wasted so just send the MOG and forget the whole dating scene." God still sent a decoy into my life that was so subtle I didn't realize it and actually thought he was the MOG. Even when I realized that he was for my preparation I still thought he was the MOG, because I didn't want to familiarize myself with any other than the one, prince. Keep all of this in mind to help safeguard your heart is the point.

Homework:

1. Make a list of characteristics of the kind of wife you think your Man of God deserves. How do you rate in comparison?

2. Have you already experience an imposter/s? How did you know he wasn't the one? How tempting was it for you to almost settle?

   Wives: Do you remember the man you dated before your husband? Remind yourself why you married your husband.

3. Now knowing about the imposter or the difference of an imposter and a decoy, do you feel better prepared? Why or why not?

   Wives: Did you experience an imposter and/or a decoy before marrying your husband?

4. Is there a possible decoy in your life now?

   Wives: Just because you're married doesn't mean Satan won't try to send a man to lure you from you husband. Write down ways to safeguard yourself from this temptation and how you can do your part to ensure your husband won't fall for this scheme.

5. Are you working on the areas needing some changes? Which areas are you working on now and which ones for the future? Tell someone for accountability and encouragement.

6. Ask yourself this great question when it's time to consider getting married. If this MOG never changed in the ways I hope he would, could I marry him "as is" and still be happy?

   Wives: Did you ask yourself this question before getting married? Regardless, you're living with your decision. Has marriage changed you or your husband? How did these changes come about?

7. After reading Genesis 29, would you say Leah was a decoy to prepare Jacob for Rachel? Why or why not?

DAPHNE M. HUNTER

Chapter 13

The Eye Opener

What can be eye opening is when others come up to you and inform you that soon you will be meeting the chosen man for you. Depending on how open you are to receive the news determines the next following steps. I remember a close friend of mine told me that and I shrugged it off, only to have my God-grandmother tell me the same thing and elaborated further about his qualities. Then things felt spooky. Weeks later a classmate that I hadn't known well told me of a dream she had of me with my new husband. She had been trying to tell me of this dream a week earlier but something always prevented her. By the time she told me, I was ready to listen, receive and accept the idea. Have you experienced a similar eye-opening situation?

You may be experiencing other eye opening situations such as, noticing the healing and restoration of your emotions, reconnecting to some past relationships and/or rediscovering some of your dreams. I didn't realize that was what was going on in my life until after these women mentioned, "Get ready for a man to enter your life." I noticed how I discovered enough healing had transformed my life to cause me to be more open to the idea, at least enough of a difference that I felt it. While you adjust to these new changes in your life you simply keep moving on with life, still not giving much thought to a prince on the horizon. That's when God will set you up.

Let's go back to discussing our prep man, the decoy,

the special agent man that God sends your way to prepare you for the Man of God. What is his purpose exactly? To help smooth your rough edges in order for the transition to be a smooth one from Mr. Imposter to our Mr. Right, the Prince. True, not everyone has a decoy, but so far I haven't found a princess that hasn't had one, if they made the decision to allow God to choose her prince. If a princess went out on her own to choose her own prince that's different. Of course, she didn't have a decoy why would she bother? There must be something to this decoy for God to send him.

Yet again, I don't know your background or what love story God has in mind for you, so I can only share from my own personal experience, so here I go again with a side note story. By the way, you'll notice I only tell you bits and pieces of my own love story and not the whole thing. Why is that? Well, one, because it is still being played out, two, because this book is about you not me – except in examples to help you.

As I was pondering the idea of what these 3 ladies told me about expecting a prince to enter my life, I made a request to the King.

"Daddy, I'm finally okay with the idea of you sending a prince of my very own. Could you please do me a favor before he comes? I know that I am not ready for him and out of much concern for him; I would like some issues to be done and dealt with before he arrives. I don't think it's fair to him to have to suffer through some of my own hang-ups. I want to be completely healed, restored and ready to start a brand new life with him to make things easier for him and me."

Daddy responded, "Some things we will take care of together, but there will be some issues that I purposefully leave undone, as I will have him be involved in your healing process."

I protested, "What for?!"

"It's my way for you to learn how to bond with him and discover how to trust him."

Does this sound familiar? Not a comforting thought, as we rather hide some of our idiosyncrasies and baggage, especially from a prince. The only thought that came to my mind was, "poor guy".

Months later, as I kept going along not expecting much of anything to happen in my life, I simply kept seeking to get closer to the King, our Daddy, God. Our relationship would deepen and He would speak to me more often until one day, God said to me:

"Your Man of God is around the corner."

"Yeah, right, you've told me he was coming "soon" before. Your definition and my definition of soon are totally different. So, what does around the corner mean?"

"It means NOW!"

I was tingling all over all day long. I was a nervous wreck. I was constantly looking over my shoulder not wanting to miss a thing. I would be at work and couldn't shake this feeling, when a recent newlywed recognized what I was experiencing. She prayed over the Man of God and me and started to prophesy over our lives. I wept as it bore witness to my spirit, and finally became calm with such a peace. Six days later I met someone. It's possible that it was my decoy.

In the meantime, God was still healing me. I didn't expect others to notice a difference. But they do notice. They don't always say anything. I guess I made enough progress for the decoy to arrive. We, princesses are well aware of our social graces and how we must keep people at a distance. This helps us keep people out and our callous hearts in. We are tough nuts to crack. Each one of us will crack differently. It could be an unexpected kind word from a gentleman or like me it started with a simple touch.

Keep in mind this wasn't just any touch; it was a resonating touch not by any passerby. This touch was innocently given on my arm by this someone. I flinched, grasped and protectively brought my arm to myself and looked at him, as if to ask, "Who are you?" Then I realized it wasn't him that touched me, but Jesus through him that did. I never felt anything like it in my life. My outer shell had a fissure and began to crack. Over the following two weeks, I had been jumpy as people came up behind me or brushed by me. I was avoiding any possible touch ever since that experience. Until I was finally confronted by a friend who helped pry open that shell for me to step out of and as a result I welcomed touch for the first time. I was living in denial. I thought I could handle being touched. I was an outgoing and touchy-feely kind of person. I mean I always asked people, "Are you huggable?" before hugging them. In that firm kingly voice God said to me, "You not only ask that to prepare them to receive your hug in touching them, you say that to prepare yourself for being touched." I never thought of that.

That first touch was an eye opener for me to realize how much healing comes from being touched. It makes sense, as we know the importance touch is to a newborn baby. Not having an intimate relationship for so long, of course I hadn't experienced touch and explained why it was so marked in my mind and heart. I went to God to discuss this, "Why was being touched and needing to be healed in this way, such a big deal?" He replied, "You need to be healed because you cannot flinch when your husband touches you."

This was the first of many stages of healing I was to go through in my preparation process with my decoy. I kept my eye on this decoy, as I wanted to see what God, the King, was up to in using him in my preparation process. I ventured out to develop a friendship with this Christian Brother since I had no idea how long he would be around in order to get me ready for my prince. I might as well get use to this guy. Perhaps the quicker I get use to the idea of him helping me get ready for the Man of God, the quicker the Man of God would come. I didn't want to prolong his arrival any longer than it had been. I had no idea how many layers of shells needed to be cracked. I thought, now that the decoy was finally here, I must be closer to meeting the Man of God than I thought...not necessarily true.

Another way the decoy can be a blessing in your healing, is to prepare you regarding how to behave around a prince. I told God, "Don't bother sending me princes to date. I'm not interested! Just make the next one the Man of God. I don't need the game playing and the aggravation!" However, at the same time I never dated as a Christian before. So, how do Christians date? If the

Christian's life is to be different from the world, dating must be too. I had no one to guide me in this area, so I sought out Christian dating books and found some to be helpful concerning guidelines, but none to tell me how to do it or what to do.

So, the first time I was asked out to an innocent lunch, I freaked out on the guy! Great Beginning! Why did I freak? One, because I told God the next guy I'd go out with would be the Man of God, how silly was that. Two, I needed the practice. However, I was concerned by going out this would be misleading to my Christian Brother. Three, why would you go out if you already had it in your heart that there is no way this could be the prince? Four, it had been a long time. What do you do? What would you say? Five, I am in a leadership position in a very visible ministry, from a well-known, respectable church. Therefore, my reputation is of great concern to me. For this reason, I have made it a point not to be seen ever alone with any man in public in order to prevent giving the wrong idea to anyone. Although it was a public place, meeting with my decoy in public was huge to me. Nothing could have prepared me for something as innocent as this. It's better to be prepared by the decoy than the actual prince.

Now for another excellent question I have been asked. As you are steadily going through your healing process as layer upon layer is being stripped off, what if the thought occurs to you that the decoy is your prince? Keep in mind the same question might have crossed your decoy's mind. Is this possible? Well, all things are possible. It could be. So, what do you do? Be still, pray and ask God, only He knows. However, He may not tell you. Keep it to yourself, put it in the back of your mind and just wait and see.

Homework:

1. What eye opening situation happened to you that made you realize that there is a prince out there for you? What happened that caused others to notice and affirm this?

   Wives: What happened that convinced you that this prince is to be your husband? Anyone else confirm to you that he was the one?

2. Were you receptive to this idea? Why or why not? How long before you were willing to accept this idea?

3. Did you make a similar request to God, the King to help you get rid of your baggage/issues before the prince comes?

   Wives: Did you feel this way? Well, baggage gone or at least reduced?

4. Do you have a decoy in your life?

5. Do you sense the time is drawing near for you to meet your Man of God? What makes you believe this?

6. Is God using a decoy or someone in your life to help tear down the walls you've built up for protection and insulation?

7. Have you established any healthy relationships with any Christian Brothers, so that it may aid you to be familiar with royal treatment? Why or why not?

8. Read the Love Story of Isaac & Rebekah in Genesis 24.

Chapter 14

The Man of God for You

As I stated in the very beginning of this book, God, our Father, the King is the biggest and most romantic person I know. He is the ultimate Love Story writer! I am going to prove just that in this chapter as I share with you my perspective of how He showed the love story of Rebekah and Isaac to me. Then we will discuss what this has to do with the Mighty Man of God for you.

Many times I have read the Bible. I've even made goals to read the entire Bible in a year and unfortunately I still haven't obtained it, yet. I prayed for God to help me, read His Word until I became engrossed and craved it. He faithfully granted my request. God met me where I was at. He knew what would catch my attention. He knew what to do, especially knowing how He made us princesses to yearn for romance. Plus, He knew it would help me be obedient to write this book. So, what did He do? He had me read Genesis 24, the Love Story that He orchestrated for Rebekah and her Prince, Isaac. (Notice, Rebekah was truly a princess, belonging to God's chosen people and Isaac being the Promised Son of Abraham meant he was truly a prince. Take courage, dear princess your promised prince is coming.)

Let me start at the beginning of my version of the Love Story between Rebekah and Isaac.

There was an amazing servant of the Lord, named Abraham who had been mourning the loss of his wife, an incredible woman of great faith named Sarah. They were the proud parents of a prince, named Isaac. Isaac wasn't just any prince. He was a Promised Prince from God Almighty. Isaac was a gift to both Abraham and Sarah for their obedience, faithfulness in serving God and for the courage they showed to dare to believe their God for a son of their own, when they both knew of Sarah's barrenness and their old age. God had proven His Word and His Promise to them and was faithful. Now it was time for Sarah to enter His rest. So, imagine the grief felt by this cherished son, knowing how his mother must have doted on him and all the countless times she told him of the story of how he came to be.

Abraham loved his son and wanted to do something to aid his son's grief and decided to seek a bride for Isaac. Not just any bride would do. He had standards; a list of qualities this bride must meet in order to be well suited for his son, a prince. He now needed a trustworthy servant to fulfill his wishes, so he called his enior servant. To ensure that his request be carried out exactly to detail, Abraham had his servant place his hand under his thigh and swear by God, the God of Heaven and Earth that he would not select a wife for Isaac from among the local girls. Instead, he would travel far and choose the girl from among God's own chosen people, she would be found in a house that served the same God.

The servant understood the seriousness of his master's request. His master was Abraham, not only a highly respected Servant of the Lord, but also a true friend of God, Himself. The servant was asked to select the Woman of God from all other women to spend her lifetime with the Promised Prince, a prince they all had waited for all these years. What a request! What pressure he felt and he had to swear before his master and God to do so. So, he asked, "But what if the woman refuses to leave home and come with me? Do I take your son back to your home country?"

Abraham replied, "Certainly not! Never! By no means are you to take my son back there. God, the God of Heaven, took me from the home of my father and from my country and gave me a promise that He would give this land to my descendants. This God will send an angel before you to get a wife for my son. If this woman refuses to come, then you are free of this oath, but whatever you do, you are not to take my son back there." So, the servant swore this oath to his master, Abraham.

The servant took 10 camels loaded down with gifts from Abraham as he traveled back to the country of Abraham's family. As he reached a city, he stopped at a well at the time the women would come to draw water for the evening. The servant prayed to the God of Heaven. "O God, God of my master Abraham, show me great success in my quest and kindness to my master by revealing to me who is the chosen bride for Isaac. Allow her to offer not only give me drink but to offer water to all 10 of my camels, too, until they have their fill. Then I'll know that you're working graciously behind the scenes for my master." Just as the servant prayed, it happened. Rebekah did this very task. The servant was stunned in silence as he wondered, "Is this her? Did God answer his prayer?" He gave her jewelry and asked her about her family, where she lived and if there was lodging. She invited him to her home.

Not only did God answer his prayer, but also there was a connection of Abraham's family with hers, his own brother's house. God went above and beyond finding a bride, all the criteria was met and then some. Rebekah was at home in a Godly house serving as expected, saving herself, learning and preparing to one day be a Godly wife and mother. She understood what it meant to be hardworking, to be compassionate to others, knowing who her people are and how to be hospitable. Her Godly traits were displayed for the servant to see not only through her hard work to serve his camels and himself, but through her heart and attitude as she willingly served. This made her equally as beautiful inwardly, not only possessing outward beauty. He knew God showed great favor to his masters, Abraham and Isaac and so he bowed and worshipped God right there.

Rebekah asked him why he was worshipping and once she found out, she told of her good fortune to her family. Her brother, Laban came to greet the servant after learning all that transpired and welcomed the servant to stay at their home. Laban had extended hospitality to his welcomed guest, but when he offered his guest a meal, the servant refused. The servant stated his reason for his journey. He explained who Abraham was and how blessed he had become. Then he told of the promised son, Isaac. He repeated his solemn oath he swore to his master before God to return to this country to find a chosen bride for Isaac. He affirmed that Isaac's wife would be well taken care of. The only way he would leave without a bride was if she refused to leave her home, people and country. Then he told his exact prayer to God upon arriving at the well and how Rebekah fulfilled his every request before he finished his prayer.

After the servant had presented the whole story to

WHEN YOU'RE READY FOR THE FAIRYTALE

Laban, don't you know Rebekah was in ear's distance to hear of what her fate would be? So, now he asked Laban, "So, what is your decision concerning Rebekah? Does she leave with me or not? I need to know my next move." Both Rebekah's father and brother knew this was obviously God's plan for her and said, "She's yours." Then the servant bowed and worshipped God yet again. He then took all the gifts he had brought and gave them to Rebekah, her mother and brother. They ate together. The servant stayed the night and was ready to leave first thing the next morning. Even being in someone else's home, the servant showed such respect as he asked to be sent back to his master, now recognizing he is a servant to Rebekah and her family. But Laban and her mother wanted her to stay 10 more days before departing, realizing she wouldn't see them again.

Instead of arguing they all agreed to allow Rebekah to make the decision of when she would depart for her new country, family and to meet her new husband. Rebekah calmly and even regally replied, "I'm ready to go." No looking back, Rebekah had been prepared, she was already looking ahead to her future, her future with Isaac, a man she didn't know, a man she hadn't met, she was prepared for her God ordained arranged marriage, she simply trusted her God like she had all her life. He had proven Himself faithful to her before, why would this be any different?

Her family took pride in her as they saw her transform from the girl they raised, to the bride of a promised prince as she prepared herself to enter her destiny. She represented them all well, as she rode like a princess with her head held high and looking radiantly as ever. They couldn't help but cry out blessings to her, for her awaiting husband and to all the future children they would be granted. Rebekah, her maids, the servant and his servants all rode off for home, her new home.

In the meanwhile, Isaac was clueless and definitely the last to know what God was up to; although, He had his best interest in mind as God, Himself was paving the way for his path to intersect with the bride of His choosing. Isaac left to visit some far off place only to return back home. He set himself to do what he normally would do, get busy working in the field. As he did, he was meditating on God; he looked up and noticed camels approaching. At that moment Rebekah's eyes met Isaac's. Rebekah knew before asking as she dismounted from her camel, but she asked anyway, "Who is that man walking to meet us?" I can imagine with a grin, the servant said, "That is my master, Prince Isaac." Rebekah respectfully covered herself with a veil, as a bride would do. Isaac stopped before Rebekah and was told of all that happened in the servant's adventure in finding Rebekah for him. At the conclusion of his story, Isaac took Rebekah's hand and gently led her to his mother's tent where he married her and loved her greatly from that day on. Only then was Isaac truly comforted from grieving his mother's death and empowered to fulfill his destiny with his Godly wife by his side.

So, what did you learn from this story in regards to yourself? First and most important, notice how great a reward it is to have a relationship with Almighty God. That God is even involved in the details of life. That He does truly care who you marry and if you trust Him enough, He will lead you right to the "chosen one for you". You can marry just anybody, but after reading and knowing you can have a love story and a romance orchestrated by God, why would you settle for less than God's best? Will God bless you and the husband you chose rather than whom He would have picked for you? Yes, of course, because you are still His princess. Would He be disappointed? In my opinion, probably, because He had better for you, but like a Father who loves unconditionally would, He would support you, love you and bless you no matter what. Next, we see how God answered the prayers of Abraham, Isaac and the servant. How He is a God of generations, of families and how He blesses our descendants. How rich He makes us in all kinds of ways! God truly not only granted Abraham his promise, but God took care of the promised son.

Faithfulness truly pays off. Abraham and Sarah were faithful to God and received their son, Isaac. The servant was faithful to Abraham in service and followed directions not only by his master, but had learned to be faithful and to depend on God, too. God was in covenant with Abraham and his household and led the servant back to a covenant keeping, God-fearing household to select "the bride" for Isaac. Rebekah was faithful in serving others and in her preparation for the day she would be found and pursued on behalf of her prince. Her family was faithful in recognizing the Hand of God on her life to release her. The servant was faithful to complete his task until finished. Isaac was faithful to be a good son to his parents. He trusted his God and in his father's choice for a bride, who would become his lifelong companion. God was faithful in covering, loving, protecting and providing for them all.

Now, God is faithful to perform our very own love

story for us, as He is no respecter of persons, if we allow and trust Him. So, let God be God. He knows what He's doing and He's good at it.

Homework:

1. Abraham established his criteria for a bride that would be a good match for his son, sound familiar? Does this help you create your own list for what you feel your Man of God deserves in you? Or even help you create a list of traits of your prince/husband?

2. Notice Abraham had the servant pursue a princess a far off on
behalf of his son and not to settle for just any girl. Why is it so important to be equally yoked with a Son of God? Are you willing to ward off the pursuit from other men in order to wait for the prince, the chosen Mighty Man of God?

   Wives: Are you equally yoked? If not, don't worry read 1 Peter 3:1-6, then invite and believe God to do a work in both you and your husband to become equally yoked. Nothing is too hard for God.

3. When asked the question, "How do you know "the one" to marry? I truly believe that you know that you know that you know; otherwise, called the Holy Spirit which will bear witness

with your spirit. But here the Holy Spirit hadn't come yet, so a sign was given. Do you believe God can still answer us with signs and miracles to confirm "the one" to us? Why or why not?

Wives: Did you believe you received a sign or confirmation that you chose the right man to marry? What was it?

4. Did you notice that Abraham and the servant discussed the future bride as "the woman" not "a woman"? They knew there was only one woman made for Isaac. That's why there was no back-up plan, such as; pick Girl "B" if Girl "A" refuses to come. In fact, Abraham said, "IF she refuses to come, then you are free from this oath." Meaning, then my son can remain single, but what faith and trust in God knowing God has someone for him and she will come. Why do you think Abraham was so confident? If Rebekah had a choice, so do you.

5. With this being the only home you have ever known, and
The servant comes for you on behalf of your Prince Isaac, are you willing to go wherever he goes? Are you willing to leave your family, neighborhood, school, work, church home, business, ministry, state or even your country for your MOG?

Wives: Did you have to give up or sacrifice anything to go and marry your husband? If so, what? If not, would you still have married your husband?

6. Abraham was adamant about his servant to never take Isaac back to his home country. God's people are never to go or look back, they only move forward. Why is that? How can this relate to you personally or even in marriage?

7. Do you think Rebekah was caught by surprise the day she was found? Do you think God warned her that the day was coming soon or that it was even that day?

   Wives: Did you have a sense the time was coming that your husband would soon enter your life?

8. Abraham trusted God for Isaac's wife. Rebekah and her
   family trusted God for a husband sight unseen. This was truly an arranged marriage. Would you be willing to trust God for a marriage like this for yourself or for your child? Why or why not?

9. Do you personally know of anyone in an arranged marriage?
   What do you think are the pros and cons of this type of marriage?

10. God was gracious enough to give confirming signs and miracles that this was the bride of His choosing for Isaac. What kind of confirming signs and/or miracles would you have to witness to feel confident that you were marrying the God ordained husband for you? Would your family have to be convinced for you to marry him or would simply you knowing be good enough for you?

    Wives: Did you receive support from your family regarding who you chose to marry? How important was this to you?

11. Isaac did love Rebekah. Do you think they had to learn to love each other over a period of time or was it soon after they met?

    Give support to your answer.

12. Simply for discussion, please look at Matthew 8:10 & verse 13. By putting our faith in God to choose our husband, would Jesus say to us what He said to the centurion?

Chapter 15

Knowing First

How many times have we heard someone tell you, "You'll just know when you meet the right person for you"? Didn't this leave you feeling like you are no more informed than when you started? How will you know? Well, as Christians we are privileged to have the Holy Spirit within us to bear witness with our own spirit, to give us the gift of discernment and to lead us into all truth. I am sure you have heard other believers say, "I know that I know that I know" when they are absolutely certain of a particular situation. Why would knowing your life partner be any different? So, having a personal relationship with the Lord Jesus Christ is one sure way of knowing who your intended spirit mate is, as long as you heed that inner witness. Remember you always have your own free will choice.

God can bring you His divine selected man into your life as long as you give Him permission to do so and are willing to do your part in the preparation process and are willing to wait on Him. Once "the prince" arrives you still have your own free will choice to accept or decline whom He has brought to you. Not only do you have your free will to be considered, but the free will of the Man of God, especially, when whom God has chosen for you may not be who you desire. Should this be the case, you will have to determine how serious you are to giving full control over to God and how truly trusting of God you are to make the most life altering decision ever.

Who should know first, the prince or the princess? Of course, every princess would say, "The prince! We want him to know first!" Most men would agree, since they are to find the damsels and women do want to be found. This answer definitely makes sense and strengthens the concept of the Men of God pursuing the Women of God.

But what if the men don't know whom to pursue? Everyone be careful who is doing the pursuing. Women are not to pursue any man, prince or not, at any time. Men need to be careful to only pursue whom God instructs; otherwise, they can be in a world of hurt or end up settling for less than God's best princess for them. The enemy wants the men to pursue the wrong princess that's his whole strategy, not God's. Satan wants you, other princesses and the Men of God, to settle for less by marrying the wrong person. It's his way to detour God's people off of God's plan for their lives, for them to suffer from being heartbroken, bored, or not fulfilling God's purpose for the both of them. If this is your experience, Praise God that Jesus came to bind up the broken hearted. You can believe for the miraculous in your relationship and remember Romans 8:28! If you are still single and tempted by the wrong MOG, why settle? When you can choose to allow God to bring you together with whom He intends and you don't have to worry if you made the right decision, you'll know you did.

Other than settling, what's another good reason to wait for your Godly spirit mate? First of all, remember God will honor the commitment you make to others and the relationships you forge with them. Especially in marriage, even if you decide to marry someone other than His choice for you. You made a vow, your words are powerful and you entered into a binding agreement called covenant, an agreement that not even death can break. Therefore, God will still bless you. However, I personally believe by allowing Him to put two people together, God provides a supernatural anointing onto such a union that when obstacles arise there is much more power to overcome them than a couple self arranged. Therefore, a person can be a good wife and/or husband, but can still be the wrong wife or husband for the person they are joined with. Eve was bone of Adam's bone and flesh of Adam's flesh. Eve was custom made for Adam. She wasn't independently created or taken from another man, she "fit" Adam and only Adam. In the last chapter, Rebekah was "the woman" for Isaac, not another. Obviously, the local girls weren't for Isaac, but all the girls at the well were princesses, but it was Rebekah who was the chosen princess and ordained by God to fit Isaac. If Abraham wasn't going to leave the bride for his promised son up for chance, why should we leave our most personal and significant relationship of our life to the odds? It all comes down to crucifying your own self-will, opinion and preferences and accepting God's will, plan and choice for your life that will best complement you in the end. Doesn't God truly know us better than we know ourselves?

Back to our question, so who should know or recognize their spirit mate first? As much as I hate to say this, more than likely it's the princess that will know long before the prince does. I will use some scripture references to support my theory. For example, read these verses in Genesis 2:15, 18, 21-22. Basically, the Lord caused a deep comatose sleep to fall on Adam and while he slept; God took one of his ribs, and designed Eve. Eve was fashioned to come alongside, to help, assist, and support the aim/goal/dream of Adam. Eve wasn't asleep, so she was "in" on what God was doing. I can imagine God telling an ever so curious Eve what His plan is as she is peeking to see who it is she needs to help. Before waking Adam, God ministers to Eve and instructs her to wait around the corner behind the trees while God arouses Adam from his slumber. Then God explains to Adam that a helpmeet, companion, friend and lover was made just for him to enjoy and now it's time for them to meet. Eve waited until God was ready to present her to him. Adam sounds awake, alert and ready to meet her (according to verse 23). This still happens nowadays, when a bride is to be well hidden behind the doors before she is escorted down the aisle to join her groom. God, Eve's Daddy brought her to the man, literally her Daddy gave His daughter, the bride away. In a wedding, a bride knows her moment is coming to be presented to her husband-to-be, whereas the groom is straining to see when is she coming?

Go back to the last chapter. Recall Isaac? What was Isaac doing while Abraham planned out the bride selection process for his son? At the end of the entire love story, who was the last to know? Isaac sure reaped the benefit of demonstrating Godly wisdom in trusting those that brought his bride to him.

Not knowing can be agonizing, remember Abraham's servant? Remember how he felt being responsible for selecting a wife for his master? He definitely wanted to know who she was without a doubt. Even after God answered his prayer, the servant still questioned it. We're no different, even when we know, we do the same thing.

Remember the part of the story where Rebekah is riding on the camel? I imagine that upon Rebekah's arrival, she notices Isaac in the field. I am sure he wasn't the only man in the field, the prince has workers out there. So, what distinguish Isaac from the others? He wouldn't be wearing his princely robes in the field to get dirty, so his clothes didn't give it away who he was. I believe the inner knowing within Rebekah told her to hone in on him as she asked the servant, "Who is that?" She simply asked for confirmation. She simply knew and then was presented to Isaac.

A little different scenario, but still proof of women knowing first; perhaps proving our female intuition is real. Let's focus on Mary and her story in Luke 1:26-38. She gives a perfect example of what I have been exhorting you to do. Which is? Mary honors and cherishes her relationship with the Lord first before any Man of God, even above her betrothed, Joseph. How do I know this? The moment Mary accepted her God assignment to birth Jesus, the Son of God, with such great faith, also knowing this meant sacrificing any hope of marriage or a future with her promised love. The scandal, the shame that would haunt her all of life of being pregnant before being married, and yet she was willing to do it alone. She knew first of the immaculate conception before Joseph was informed. Joseph was already looking for a way out, to divorce her privately, but God sent an angel to set him straight, to follow His plan. (Matthew 1:18-25) Like Abraham, Mary sacrificed her promise, but God restored her fiancée back to her as God gave Isaac back to Abraham. (As an interesting note, what connects these 3 romances, Adam & Eve, Rebekah & Isaac and Mary & Joseph? That they are the only 3 couples that mentions

God, Himself responsible for putting them together.) Then when Mary went to visit her cousin, Elizabeth, Elizabeth knew Mary was pregnant before Mary could tell her. (Luke 1:39-45) You will find Mary knowing first again, in John 2:1-10. Mary knew it was time for Jesus' first miracle before the disciples.

Women know timing, even if they may not know exactly the what, when, or who; however, they perceive it is soon. Don't worry, princess, upon God's timing, He will inform you, too.

Why? Why would God tell His daughters of the right prince for them before telling His sons? One, because His daughter, the princess is so precious to Him, that her heart is a treasure and it's not to be trifled with. Two, He knows how He made His girls to complete a prince and how soft their hearts are and how easily they can fall in love. So knowing aids them in protecting their hearts from the wrong prince and only willing to open their heart to the right one.

It's not so bad knowing first, the hard part is waiting for the prince to wake up and realize it himself. This is a test. This phase is very similar to that of being encased in chapter 2. As the princess is waiting for the light to go on in his head, she is wringing her hands and asking the King, "Daddy, what's going on? Why doesn't he get it? Why doesn't he know that I am standing right before his very eyes?" She is met with silence. The enemy comes to deceive, sabotage and cause doubt like he did in a garden long ago with the original princess named Eve. He caused her to doubt God by asking, "Is this really your prince? What makes you think so? Did God really tell you he's your prince or did you make it up?" Don't listen to him. Wait for a word from God. Keep holding onto the promise given long ago. Keep hoping for some sign of confirmation. Once you receive a confirmation whether big or small, you still end up asking yourself, "Was that really a confirmation? Is Daddy doing this to encourage me to hold on and wait? Am I reading into this? Is this all in my head?"

You may or may not receive any definitive answers to these questions, but journaling will help. If you journal long enough a pattern will form and perhaps your answer will be right in front of your face. Another way to reach an answer is to wait on God. Simply stand and wait on Him to tell you what to do next. Put that area of your life on hold, just pause everything. Often He only tells you what to do one step at a time. Last but not least, you simply wait on the prince to come to his senses and once he gets the green light, he will approach you or even better he will pursue you.

Here are some questions I've been asked.

1) What if I know and I think he knows?
   Then wait for the prince to bring it up to you, let him take the lead of the budding relationship. You might think he knows and really he is clueless. Let God bring it up to him.

2) What if he knows that I know?
   Same answer, wait on him to take the initiative.

3) What if I know and God is telling me to tell him?
Stand and make absolute sure that God is telling you to tell him. Only in rare occasions have I seen where this is the case, but it has happened. For example, the Biblical reference of when Ruth waited at Boaz' feet. He noticed her, he inquired about her, he approached her, but once the harvest season was over, he did nothing. Her last chance was up, it was a now or never situation and Ruth only did so in obedience to Naomi. Only do so in obedience to God.

4) What if we both know, what do we do now?
Well, once it is confirmed that you do in fact both know that God has brought you together here are a few accounts I've witnessed how others handled this, but you both need to pray, seek God and do a lot of talking regarding what is right for the both of you.

a) One couple got married right away saying, "Why wait when we know its God?"

b) Another couple began to date to get to know each other and 3 weeks later they were engaged.

c) Yet another couple joined a ministry together to get to know each other by working on a project together, then dated and ended up getting married.

5) What's the difference between a soul mate and a spirit mate?

A soul mate is who you would choose out of your wants, desires and preferences to satisfy your physical, mental and emotional needs. Whereas your spirit mate is handpicked by God, to meet all your needs, the most important of these being your spiritual needs first and foremost. Then the mental, emotional and physical needs fall into place and are greatly enhanced and quenched, phenomenally.

Homework:

1. How would you feel if God brought you someone that isn't your type? Would you be willing to stay the course?

2. God didn't need a Christian Dating Service. So what do you think of these? What would you say if someone suggests that you sign up and try it? Would you join? Why or why not?

3. How do you feel about possibly knowing who your Man of God is before he knows?

4. There are 2 definitions of "settling". The first is, if you are too impatient to wait on God to bring you your prince, so you quit and enter a relationship of your choosing. The second is if you actually wait on God and refuse to accept who He brought you and choose a mate of your own. Either way, are you willing to settle?

5. Do you know of a love story where someone knew before the other person? How did it turn out? How does this effect what you would do if it was you?

Chapter 16

Preparation

After all of this, how do you actually prepare for meeting the Mighty Man of God? How do you prepare for marriage? Is there such a thing? I believe there is, it all depends on how serious you are about the most important commitment in your life other than to your Lord and Savior, Jesus Christ.

First of all, the best thing you can do is, spend a lot more time with God. Further develop your relationship with Him. He should be your number one relationship. In fact, the closer you get to Him the closer you get to your Man of God. Envision a pyramid with God at the top of the vortex, you at the base of one slope and the MOG at the base of the other. You both steadily move up towards God as you seek Him first and then you find each other. I'll never forget the morning, I woke up and my first thoughts were of God and how grateful I was for our relationship. Then He surprised me with this comment, "Daphne, don't move, stay where you are. I'm almost ready to present you." I knew He was referring to my side of the slope, my Man of God is steady coming up and just about there to meet me. How encouraging was that? God knows my heart is after Him. (Psalms 37:4 & Matthew 6:33)

Next, find out what does being a wife mean? Ask God to teach you and sho how to be a wife. Ask Him to reveal to you the kind of wife He wants you to be and the kind your Man of God deserves.

God is faithful to answer you. He will even disclose the list of desirable traits your husband-to-be has created for his dream wife. You may not meet all of them, but you have something to strive for. Then it is up to the Man of God if he is willing to accept you the way you are. If he doesn't, don't be disappointed as it isn't his place to change you that is left up to God. He is only to accept and love you whether you meet all his expectations or not. Remember if he can't accept you, then he must not be your Man of God after all. The same goes for you regarding him, too. Keep in mind we all have areas that we need to grow in, improve and build on. If God tells you this is your MOG, with or without your desired changes, that's where trust in God comes in. God must certainly know something that you don't, including knowing that this man will meet needs you didn't know you had. Who knows both of you better than God?

Another thing that bothers me is, people go to college and study to earn degrees for a better career, but don't adequately prepare for such a major decision of their life, such as marriage. So, where do you begin to prepare for marriage? The Bible, since God is the originator of marriage, let's see what His Word has to say about it. I suggest an in-depth study of The Song of Solomon in the Bible. Also, reading other books, watching marriage seminar videos/DVDs, attending marriage workshops, interviewing successful marriage couples, etc. are good places to start.

Then there are those of us that want to plan everything. We make lists of items we want to take care of before getting married in order to become a better person for oneself and our future spouse. This list can be a healthy start to righting some wrongs or dealing with areas of your life that have been left undone. Be sure not to put unnecessary pressure on yourself by making unrealistic expectations to get them all completed as you never know when the Man of God shows up. Take care of these issues for you and not just for the prince.

Emotional preparation may include dealing with past relationships. For example, before having a relationship with your husband, you may need to confront, re-establish, heal or consider your relationship with the first man of your life, your father. Perhaps there are other significant male relationships you held in your life that you need to deal with. Even restoration within your family such as with a long lost brother or sister, those relatives you haven't seen or spoken to in awhile. Why would you consider doing this? When a couple decides to marry it's not just each other that they marry, but they marry each other's family, too. It's important to know where you're from and who your people are. Abraham knew his as he sent his servant back in search for Rebekah. Then Rebekah gave her lineage upon request by the servant, which was confirmation that God led him successfully. Knowing your family gives a sense of knowing who you are.

It was already discussed about having a confidence rooted in Christ. This is usually dependent on how you feel about yourself. I don't believe you can have this amazing confidence of who you are in Christ if you haven't established the love you have for Jesus or yourself. If you find it difficult to love yourself, spend a lot of time with Jesus and His Word and you will learn how He sees you and then you will see yourself the same way He does. As the Bible says, "...You shall love your neighbor as yourself"

(Matthew 19:19). If you don't love or care for yourself how can you love and care for your husband? Or why should he love and care for you? You are important. You must take care of you, as you are and will be the heart of the home and are expected to take care of all the others in relation in your household.

Mental preparation may include rearranging your priorities. With life's busy schedules, there's never enough of time for all the people in your life, let alone yourself or for all the activities. I've had to learn to slow down, count the cost, see what really matters, change some things, give up others and readjust my pace in order to appreciate what God has given me. It wasn't easy for me and don't expect it to be for anyone else, but it is very necessary. As they teach in church, God is a God of order and proper priorities and here is the list according to importance. Maintain your relationship with God first and foremost, next will be with your husband once he comes, then your children if you have any, job/career, ministry or other commitments and (God) dreams/aspirations. If you keep these in proper perspective and check on them regularly you shouldn't go wrong. If you mess up, get back to the basics and just be teachable or someone who loves you will have to remind you of this.

While you are getting organized and once the time comes, get ready to merge your things with his things and consider some of these thoughts. What is really important for you to keep, that you can't do without? What would be nice to start collecting together? God told me to go through and get rid of some stuff because why would I want to take anything from my past that was dead and bring it into the new life He was preparing for me? He was doing a new thing in me, through me and for me. Didn't I perceive it? You count the costs. The Man of God is worth it. Another thing God was telling me was I needed to become portable. I know the call on my life includes travel eventually. I never know when, so why not start preparing now?

To alleviate mental stress is to deal with and become financially prepared, if possible. Nowadays, people have a lot of debt. This is an area you may want to start working on. I know I want to be an asset, a benefit, a blessing to my husband. There's things I want to get a handle on so that once we come together we both know where we will stand and what financial goals we need to set. I know I want to give more to the Kingdom of God to see His gospel cover the earth, but before I can do that I need to be a good steward and become debt-free first. We all would love to be debt-free or lessen the number of liabilities we have upon entering our Heaven sent relationship, but more than likely that is not going to happen. So, don't let Satan beat you up. Find out what you can do and start where you're at and don't forget to always tithe so that God can rebuke the devourer of your finances!

As far as your personality is concerned, be more open and approachable. If you're not, then how do you expect your Man of God to come up to you? Learn to be comfortable with yourself and help others feel comfortable in your presence. This may take more time depending on the severity of the hurt you have undergone and how much healing you have already experienced. Instead of just casual interaction, you must come to a point of letting your guard down to let others get behind the wall. This allows them to get to know you and allows you to get to know others. This is good as it will help you develop a support network of friends. This will be healthy for your marriage, as it will take the unrealistic expectation off of your husband from trying or having to be everything to you. Outside relationships will help meet your other social needs and keep you looking forward to seeing your husband and him wanting to be with you.

Then there's physical preparation. Let's begin with your self-image. I saved this one for last on purpose because I know how we women are. We will always find something wrong with ourselves. Whether, it's our hair, complexion, body shape, weight, etc. Remember two things. One, you are made in God's image, just the way you are right now and two, if you are truly that unhappy with yourself, then do something about it. You shouldn't complain if you did it to yourself. Again, stop beating yourself up and don't give a chance to the enemy to do the same. Simply write down in your journal what your issue is, your goal, what you're going to do about it and when. After doing that you will have a sense of gaining control and it won't feel as overwhelming.

Another area that concerns us is being sexually prepared. Don't think God doesn't care about you being prepared sexually. He does. I know it sounds hard to believe. From time to time, your body will awaken to sexual desires again. These desires will be a shock if you haven't experienced them for a significant length of time. Since you have been quite functional without these dormant desires, but when you experience your first brief "awakening" women have expressed such feelings as, guilt, shame, confusion, condemnation, etc. Why? They believe they have disappointed God by allowing these feelings to resurface. There is no need to feel this way as God created you and these desires, so you are not sinning.

Before I continue any further, I want to address those of you, who have already engaged in premarital sexual activity, do not feel condemned. When you invited Jesus into your heart and life, He forgave you of all of your sins including sexual sin. If you do not have a relationship with Jesus, you can refer to page 157 and then complete the enclosed card. If you do have a relationship with the Lord, stop allowing the enemy and/or yourself to rehearse your past and hinder you from moving forward. After accepting Jesus and confessing your sin, your guilt and condemnation has and will continually be washed away.

Pray with me.

Jesus, I come to you now because although you tell me my sins have been forgiven, I haven't forgiven myself. My regrets, my memories my guilt, my shame keep taunting me. I don't feel worthy of you especially with all I'm learning about you and how you really love and see me. I'm learning of the kind of woman, wife and mother you want me to be and it's beyond me, but I do want my life to change and with your help I know I can. Please show me, help me to embrace your work in me. Help me to change, love, and forgive myself so I can follow you more easily and be ready for the gift of a Man of God you have predestined for me. I pray my MOG is able to forgive and embrace me regardless of my past as I will his. Thank you, Lord, in your mighty name I pray, amen.

Whether we enter a Godly Covenant Marriage as a virgin or have been forgiven and renewed. The purpose of sex is to become "one" with your husband. These "awakened" desires happen for two reasons. Reason one, to prepare you for the right time, making you willing and to maximize your pleasure. Waiting to have such desires all of a sudden on your honeymoon night would cause much more anxiety. Reason two, it is your spirit recognizing and "longing" to be joined with its spirit mate. Your spirit knows the time is drawing near to be "one". So, don't confuse your "longing" for lust or loneliness. How beautiful is that? Isn't it incredible, how your spirit recognizes him before your own natural mind or eyes do? What more do you need to prove that you are a spirit being? It's your spirit that confirms "the one" to you.

After explaining the "longing" desires a woman feels, I was asked "Does the prince experience these "longings"? I don't know; however, since we are told men think of sex more often than women do, perhaps, they wouldn't notice the difference in their fleshly sexual desires and the "awakening" of their spiritual desire to want to be "one" with their princess. I'd like to believe they do. I can't imagine God holding out on them this incredible expression of readiness to please their wife. Perhaps this is God's way of letting the princes know it's not good for them to be alone and that He gave them these desires so they aren't sinning, like we're not. Remember God gives only good gifts to His children and sex is one of those gifts.

The beautiful part of lovemaking with your husband is not only a personal, intimate encounter with one another but it is a form of worship to God. He smiles upon the both of you seeking oneness, while a bond is being formed between the 2 people He loves and adores so much that trusted Him to purposefully bring you both together. Imagine God's prospective. For example, it's almost like when you give someone a really great gift and you can't wait to see their expression when they open it up because you know they are going to love it! What better gift than giving yourself completely to your husband and himself to you? This thought gives more meaning to the scripture found in Ecclesiastes 4:12, "...a threefold cord is not easily broken."

Lovemaking is a gift and it pleases God. The Bible says in Hebrews 13:4, "the marriage bed is undefiled." I mention this because of varying questions regarding what is permissible in lovemaking before God. The answer depends on the husband and wife. Whatever both are comfortable with is acceptable, but as long as one is uncomfortable than it's not okay before God. Other perverse suggestions such as, multiple partners, pornographic material or other sexual sin is obviously out of the question as it is not okay with God; therefore, it shouldn't be permitted nor considered by either of you.

Now knowing that lovemaking with your husband is a form of worship to God. You wouldn't intentionally withhold any other forms of worship from God, so don't withhold sex from your husband. To do so, would be considered selfish, especially when your body is no longer your own. When you entered a relationship with God for His reasonable service and then you willingly give yourself over to your husband when you pledge your wedding vows your body became his and his body became yours. (1 Cor. 7:3-4) There is nothing stronger than the sexual bond with your husband. Why would you weaken the intimacy shared between the both of you?

This is where my passion stems for you and why I

had to ultimately write this book for you. My deepest heart's desire is for you <u>not</u> to settle for what the world offers as a means to finding your husband but to trust God in bringing you to your husband!

One last thing that you need to know as part of your preparation is about the preparation your husband must undergo. Always keep in mind that the King, your Daddy is working on his son, the prince, not just on you. When it's time for you both to come together, you both will be ready. Although, I can't tell you much about what the prince's preparation entails. I can tell you there is a difficult season you must endure before he is ready and you're presented. There is a period of separation. This particular season of being separated can happen at anytime in your getting to know one another stage. I've seen it in the beginning, mid-way and at the very end. After some time is spent sharing thoughts, experiences, feelings, and there's a recognizable connection between you and the prince, it can freak out one or both of you. I don't know what exactly freaks out the person. Perhaps it's the realization of knowing that this is the person for you for the rest of your life. Allow me to share with you some instances from a couple of my friends' lives.

I prayed with this dear friend of mine, (who was a single mom) for her MOG. God showed me instantly who her MOG was while praying, but I never told her, it wasn't my place to tell. It was for God to reveal it to her and to him. Now looking back, I understand why God allowed me "in" on their relationship from the beginning. It started with a simple prayer request that will last for all eternity. God had me share with her all that I am telling you to do in this book. She started journaling to her MOG, even while having a suspicion that she may know who the MOG might be. She told me who she thought her MOG was, unknown to her inside my mind I'm screaming, "YES, IT IS!!!"

When it was about 2.5 years into getting to know each other, they had never dated, yet the princess knows how she feels for this prince, out of the blue the prince disappears for 6 months! No explanation, no goodbye, nothing! Leaving the princess bewildered! She called me with horrible negative thoughts as she was trying to grasp for reasons he would drop out of her life. What did she do? Did she offend him by saying or doing the wrong thing? Was it another girl that took him away? After the 6 months, he returned and re-entered her life like nothing happened. This princess didn't prod him for any explanation; she had to readjust to him. She guarded her heart, yet still loved him. Another 6 months went by and then he was ready to tell her how he felt about her for the first time in 3 years. He nervously shared that he had to spend alone time with God during that time to search his heart, and allow God to deal with his heart, train him and grow him up to become the husband and father he would need to be. His biggest hang up wasn't the role or the responsibility. His heartfelt concern is felt in his words. "Father, this princess you've brought to me is so exquisite! What a gift? I don't deserve her. How could I? What does she see in me? She's incredible! Her personality, character, she's a great mother, friend and knows how to pray! Not to mention how stunningly beautiful she is. Why would she choose me? Why would you choose me? She can do so much better than me!" Once he gave his insecurities to God, God returned him back to His daughter a new man. Then he explained to her how God had transformed him and now he knows who he is and that she is who he loves, and he ended his confession with a marriage proposal. They had their first date 2 weeks later and 8 months later they finally came together and entered into the destiny that God had planned for their lives on August 13, 2005 when the two became one.

Another story is of two really great friends from school, they go to the same church and in ministry together. They simply loved to hang out with each other. Then one day it turned into something more for her as God had to "turn on the light" for her to see it. She thought, "No Way!" It was too perfect, but knew once he knew, it would be smooth sailing! They knew everything about the other, so of course! This was definitely God! He agreed to meet her for dinner and she carefully told him all that God has revealed to her. In complete shock, he thought she lost her mind and told her so! He said, "I think you're hearing voices or something, because it can't be God! He's my God, too and He didn't tell me!" They left. She went to God, "What happened?!" For 3 months, he no longer communicated with her and she was his best friend. His response was complete and total avoidance. All she had was God to comfort her as she cried all her tears out to Him. In that time, he too went to God. "God, I don't know where she is coming from saying you've chosen us to be together as husband and wife? You need to talk to your daughter! Here I am, God, talk to me. She's my best friend, how do I handle this? Is this true?" Then God confirmed his daughter's words to the prince. The prince's heart was heavy. "Oh, God! Why didn't you tell me? You told her, but didn't tell me. Why didn't you talk to me first? The prince realized because he wouldn't have listened or accepted it. He had his own expectations of who he wanted. He was only on the lookout for his idea of who "she" should be and not who God put before him. Then his thoughts went to his best friend. "Oh, God, what I've done to her heart. I miss her." He returned to her and made things right. Even with others trying to talk him out of it, no one could because he heard from God and he knew how much they had grown together unknowingly. He was ready to enter into covenant with her. Today their love story gives such hope to other princesses that "know first". Even greater hope comes out of seeing how God has blessed them in their marriage, their family, and their ministry. God is so good!

What I've been told, during this time of separation, is to encourage the princesses to "Be Still and Let God Be God" to the prince. Do not initiate communication with the prince in any form as God will deal with him and possibly still dealing with you. Continue to be in constant prayer for God's will and His timing.

Homework:

1. How is your relationship with God? Are you getting sidetracked from God by focusing too much on your MOG/husband?

2. Have you discovered what kind of wife God needs you to be? The kind your MOG/husband needs?

3. Have you begun your preparation process? If so, what have
you done so far? Has it been easy or difficult?

4. Has this chapter given you any ideas where to start or what to add to your list?

5. What areas do you need to further develop in order for your future/marriage to be healthy?

6. What other suggestions could you offer that weren't listed?

7. Start dreaming with God again. Write down the vision of your wedding day or to renew your vows. (Hab.2:2-3)

Chapter 17

The Virgin Complex

I never would have thought that I would suffer from the "Virgin Complex". First of all, what is it? Having a complex can mean a number of things. In the way I choose to describe it, the following definition fits; an exaggerated reaction to the subject of sex. A complex also means the way an individual thinks or feels intently and it influences their attitudes and behavior. So, do you get the picture? Being a virgin, how do you feel about sex? What myths have you heard? What makes you so curious about what it will be like when it finally happens? What are you looking forward to experiencing? What are you afraid you might discover? It's interesting how some of these questions don't only apply to first time virgins, but they re-surface in spiritual virgins, too.

Naturally, in our cultural way of thinking, a virgin is a person who has not experience sexual intercourse. You would be right. However, there are more definitions to what a virgin can also mean as long as you are open to abstract definitions. For example, we use the word "virgin" for a person who hasn't experienced something other than sex. Another example would be to order a drink without alcohol in it would be called a virgin (margarita, daiquiri, etc.). I mention this to introduce an idea that never occurred to me until my spiritual mama was exhorting me to keep believing God for a husband despite my divorce and past. Then her face lit up as she proudly announced, "Daphne, it just hit me! You have never dated as a Christian before. You've been married, but you were unequally yoked and that was before you became a Christian. That means you're a "Spiritual Virgin!" A what?! I didn't know if I should be embarrassed or elated. She went onto tell me how everything is "different" including sex when you really trust God to bring the MOG to you.

Ever since that conversation, I gave more thought to being a spiritual virgin and discovered things about myself. I guess I hadn't noticed until she put a label on me. When she pointed it out, I instantly blushed and my newfound innocence resurfaced. It had been there all along just had been undetected. Before when I was in the world I knew how to recognize when a man would be interested or attracted to me, how to flirt, etc., now I was utterly clueless. Friends would have to tell me, "He likes you or he's flirting with you." I was completely oblivious. By the time I noticed with their help, it was too late to encourage the guy, if I wanted to, but I never wanted to. My friends just laughed at me and labeled me hopeless.

Then of course your mind begins to wander and imagine when the MOG does arrive and it's your first time what will that experience be like and it makes you extremely nervous. Not that there's anything to be nervous about. Why be nervous prematurely? Meaning there's not even a Man of God insight, so there's plenty of time. However, that excuse doesn't curb the anxiety. Oh brother, no one warns you about having to dispel those kinds of fears. I mean how ridiculous is that?! For example, I have children, there's not much I don't already know. Believe it or not that doesn't matter. The whole idea of being a spiritual virgin equates to the same anxieties of being an actual virgin in the natural. Your imagination runs wild with all kinds of thoughts.

I did my best to curb my mind's wonderings and when I thought I had it all under control I would stumble into situations or conversations that would reintroduce the topic. While in the ladies dressing room, I overheard a newly engaged young lady sharing her fears about the Honeymoon night to the other women. I couldn't help but be torn within myself as I heard her anxiousness and the answers given to her by those who were married. She wondered if sex would be enjoyable upon the first attempt only to be met with such answers as, "No, you learn to like it" or "It's nothing like you think it will be" or "I couldn't believe how much it hurts." I was surprised at how none of the answers sounded positive. On one hand, her question had been my own. "Would sex with my MOG be enjoyable from the beginning because of the reverence I shown the Lord in waiting for the right husband?" Then I was deflated by the women's answers. I almost wanted to speak up in a more reassuring way to the young lady, but who was I to say anything when I obviously got it all wrong and ended up divorced. I know that's a ridiculous thought since she just wanted someone to share regarding their "experience" but that's just it, my experience had only been with a non-believer. Unlike me, she was a natural virgin who had waited and was to marry a MOG. However, her honeymoon experience would turn out, I knew her experience would outdo mine simply because she would be equally yoked, whereas I wasn't and suffered; therefore, that's why I had nothing to offer her in reassurance. Little known to her, she probably would have more to share with me afterwards while I am still on my journey of singleness.

Upon becoming a princess, a lot of habits changed and a significant one was how I dressed. I don't even remember how it came about, but modesty goes hand in hand with reputation, poise, mannerisms and self-worth. I couldn't believe how being more selective of my clothing directly affected the level of respect I gained from others. Their respect and positive affirmations affected my behavior and reinforced the right habits. I didn't really wear revealing outfits at all, but what I did wear made me noticeably uncomfortable to be seen wearing it; although, at the time I couldn't explain or know why. Then I didn't have much of a sense of style. That soon changed and my style developed based on my modesty, comfort and function. Then my style appeared and it suited me.

My next episode of being innocent came with the avoidance of media. With everything on TV and in the movies it all seemed to focus on sex. I couldn't stand to see any of it. I don't watch TV at all now, mostly due to my hectic schedule but there's nothing worth watching. I believe there's truth to the Sunday school song "Be careful little eyes what you see." In defending my choice to abstain from such garbage on the Big Screen I was mocked for being "prude". The jeering hurt, not because of my convictions but because of being labeled such an outdated term. Who uses that word anymore? I felt old. Which leads to a completely different fear, the fear of being too old to get married or being a single mom and who would want someone with kids? Don't worry God knows all of that and yet He still has someone just for His girls.

That's reassuring, but not enough to dispel the fears of being older than your typical single young woman. What about hating yourself for no longer having the figure you had prior to having kids. Then there's the feeling the need to compete with what the culture promotes as what is beautiful and you know you're nothing close in comparison. It's normal to feel like this as all women have feelings of inadequacy. Maybe from a comment made by family or a close girlfriend and what was said has stuck with you. Then there's the dress you hate because it looks better on someone else than you. So this carries over into if you're not happy while dressed then you're probably definitely not pleased with yourself while undressed. You figure if you're not, then he won't be either. Like everything else, you can overcome this! How? By your level of confidence and simply being yourself, be the one he fell in love with, so much so he will propose and marry you.

If that's not enough, once you manage to overcome that obstacle you move onto worrying about the mechanics of sex. Will your bodies complement each other? For spiritual virgins a worry that comes up, is will the MOG be wondering or worrying about previous sexual relationships his princess had or vice-versa? What if a former sin of your MOG was pornography and thoughts nag you about it in the back of your mind. See what sin has done? It has robbed you of being anxiety free while enjoying your God given mate for life. Remember all sin, his and yours is from the past and has been covered by the blood of Jesus. Jesus has forgiven and forgotten and you both should, too. Jesus made all things new, believe and receive the brand new gift of you, the new love you found and the new experiences of sharing yourself unlike ever before.

When does intimacy grow? Long before it's time

for sex, actually intimacy is scarier than sex. Intimacy is the uncovering of the soul more than just being undressed. Intimacy should be read as – "Look...into me, see?" It's the sharing of your heart, telling of secrets, dreams, childhood stories, self discoveries, hopes for the future, memories made together and the enjoyment of each other's company so much so that you don't want to go on with life without the other. Then when a declaration of both hearts' desire is to share life together as one, then the intimacy already experienced is just further enhanced by the coming together sexually. The oneness shared beforehand should dispel any hindrances from disrobing.

Like I said before, God gives only good gifts to His children and sex is one of those gifts. He saved you and the MOG to come together as husband and wife only to have the two of you un-wrap each other and to share in the joy that sex brings. He invented sex and is present as you unwrap your 'gift" and enjoy each other. Your joy and fulfillment brings Him joy because He loves you and your MOG so much. When you follow His will, His plan, His way and it makes you happy then it makes Him happy, too.

A very important thing to know, remember and consider is having sex (or if you prefer to call it making love) is a form of worship to God. Worship is typically the word used when singing in church. Maybe comparing sex to music isn't a bad idea, as an old flirtatious saying would be, "Let's make beautiful music together." Those that enjoy creating music, become one with their instrument as they develop their talent or create a "new sound". By practicing with the instrument of their choice, they discover a new form of expression of themselves as their music reflects an intimate experience. This could compare to an indescribable sense of oneness found out of intimacy experienced with another.

The man is given a leadership role by God. Therefore, the man should be leading the romance all along, including leading his bride into the presence of God. Whenever God is invited He makes everything better and richer. If God dwells and walks among His people, then why wouldn't He want to be included in the ultimate celebration? Sex is the pinnacle of coming together of His son and daughter whom He's chosen to unite in the most passionate and intimate way. God created this gift to be enjoyed. In fact, He made it a point to be so intimate that humans are the only ones to experience sex face-to-face.

Like everything else, the enemy is consistent to steal our enjoyment of our gift of sexual intimacy. Whether he corrupts are minds from things we see, hear or remember from our past or cause disappointment in what we are in hopes to experience. Proving John 10:10 to be true yet again, which states, "The thief's purpose is to steal and kill and destroy. My purpose is to give them a rich and satisfying life." Don't let the enemy steal your sexual satisfaction, kill your intimacy or destroy your marriage! Even if you manage to be free of such mental garbage, he will thwart you with feelings of inadequacies if not before sex then perhaps afterwards. Again, Don't Let Him! Be on your guard. We are told to cast down any evil imagination that tries to exalt itself above what God says.

Think about it. Isn't it funny how the enemy manipulates you along with your own fleshly mind, will, emotions, and desires to entice you to have sex before marriage? Why does he do it? To steal the opportunity of fulfilling God's plan, His will and His way of doing things to prevent you from feeling secure and having the most joyful, rich and satisfying sex life possible. The Deceiver, along with our stirred up emotions and desires, makes temporary passion look like long-lasting love, but it's far from it. As long as we don't succumb to our lust and impatience we will have God's plan, His will and His way. The enemy wants to destroy the beauty of ultimate oneness in the atmosphere of purity and freedom as intended by God, your Father, your Daddy, and the King. Sex is God's Love Gift to you through His Man of God for you and to bring both you and him intense pleasure. This is what God has chosen for you, not the atmosphere of secrecy and dirty shame to be hidden in the dark that causes regret and will lessen what was to be experienced. Sex is addicting because craving intimacy is natural. If premarital sex continues it will only bring loads of condemnation, shame, regret, and feeling dirty each time. With each experience it will continually be added to the pile that darkens the heart and mind and pollutes the spirit. Then to dismiss it we try something "new" or "kinky" to rid the heap and fulfill the ache for that excitement once experienced but it only furthers the downward spiral. If the enemy gets you to do it once he will get you to do it again. Even worse, he will give you sinful thoughts to bring into your marriage later. Now creating fear, wounds, hurt, struggles and impure thoughts to spoil the fruit of your entire relationship with your husband and it will manifest in the bedroom, unless fought off early on.

Do you think the enemy stops once you're married now that sex is an "allowed" norm? Oh No! He is just getting started. Now, he works doubly hard to prevent sex from happening at all. Sex is more than a physical act, it's powerful, it keeps you intimately connected to your husband and to God; therefore, it is spiritual warfare. Doesn't that make sense? With two opposing forces fighting, meaning at war, wouldn't the same form of weapons be used? It's all a matter of who the weapon is pointing at. When we side with God it's a direct hit at the enemy. When our perverted imaginations, actions and/or withholding of sex from our husband gets the better of us, we side with the enemy; therefore, we not only hit God we actually hurt ourselves more. God's only hurt because we hurt, he shares our pain due to His great love for us. When there are times that you and the hubby want to roll to opposite ends of the bed. Guess who is laying with elbows crossed behind his head with plenty of room and blanket getting all comfortable in between? The enemy called Division. Refuse to sleep with the enemy!

There is another enemy who seeks to wreak havoc in your marriage, she's called Discord. She's married to Division. She notices everything and brings it to your attention. If you had sex prior to marriage she will point out how different sex is after marriage, as if it is disappointing. It's NOT!! It's different from anything you have ever experienced because you finally did it right. You have only known what it is like the wrong way. It feels different because it's your legal benefit to being married. No sneaking, no hiding and no secrets. Then she lays low while you adjust to married life. Sex is often at the beginning and then your lives take over and intimacy becomes neglected. This can and should be avoided. Sex needs to be often. Why? Out of respect and to meet the needs of your husband, both of them. While you were single, God was your husband. (Isaiah 54:5) As I said before, sex is worship to God and worship is required often. Worship keeps you spiritually and intimately connected to God therefore, this intimate, physical act keeps you connected to your Man of God. As you keep the MOG needs met in this area he will keep your needs met for feeling loved. However, for whatever reason if sex takes the back burner and the relationship is lacking in another area for whatever reason. Discord returns. Her voice is aided by what you see and hear from the TV, movies, disgruntled girlfriends, your own disappointments, frailties, inadequacies, etc. So now she nags you about what your husband use to do and why doesn't he do it lately? She begins to compare your husband to others whether onscreen or in real life only making you fearful and unhappy until it may drive you to actually repeat her nagging to your husband. Don't Do This!! Stop waiting for your husband to do something! You're the other half of the marriage. Let the cycle end with you. Begin anew and be creative! There is a law of cause and effect. Be caring towards yourself and your husband. Find out what's causing the effect you're feeling. Stop thinking of you and find out is something bothering your husband. Have you stopped doing something that is appealing to him? Perhaps, there is no reason at all, just time for something new between you two and Division and Discord aren't invited!

Please do not get me wrong, sex is not the power of your marriage, it is simply the follow through. God should and has been your source in your singleness and still should remain the source while married. This makes Him the power that holds your marriage together. Keep your focus on God, obeying and pleasing Him and you will see the result of a powerful marriage. Such results are, love, respect, gentleness, tenderness, understanding, forgiveness, longsuffering and intimacy. Therefore, do not be ignorant of the enemy's evil schemes whether before or after your fairytale commitment comes. Overcome evil with good and hopefully with some good healthy sex!

All of this is why remaining a virgin or being sexually pure/abstinence is so important. You protect yourself from unnecessary heartache and in doing so prove you thought so highly of your husband and marriage in advanced to reap your due reward in the end. What a victory to beat the enemy by choosing God and His best plan for you! Remember if for whatever reason you fell in the moment and passion overtook you once or repeatedly. There is now, at this very moment, no condemnation for those that belong to Christ. He has forgiven those that have confessed their sin to Him and decide to no longer go in that direction. Forgive yourself. Remember God is and always has been a carpenter that means He knows how to fix the unfixable. He builds and restores everything even better than its original condition. How? He does so by creating the new spiritual virgin within you while you travel the single journey of preparation. Also, if married and have fallen to the devices of Division and Discord, again STOP! Confess to God. Ask for you and your marriage to be restored. Forgive yourself and let God begin the reconstruction between you and your husband.

Homework:

1. Was the concept of a "Spiritual Virgin" a new one to you? What do you think about it?

2. Have you experienced your own anxiousness concerning sex? Combat anxiety by meditating and/or discussing these scriptures: Proverbs 12:25 and Philippians 4:6

3. What advice would you like to be given if you were that recently engaged woman? What advice would you give if you had the opportunity?

4. Have you notice a change in your "modesty" since beginning this journey? Your clothes, make-up, media choices? Yes, or no and how? If so, how do your new changes make you feel? Why do you think you weren't like this before? Are there any other changes you've made not listed here? If so, what are they?

5. What "thought-attacks" have wounded you that compel you to feel unworthy or inadequate of a Man of God and hinder you of wanting to be sexually intimate?

6. If concerned about the "sexual mechanics" that's what honesty is about. Intimacy is found in those talks. So be open to share and be comfortable with the MOG. He will appreciate this and not having to be a mind-reader. I'm sure he much rather know he's bringing you pleasure than you saying nothing and just grin and bearing through it. Remember you are only missing out on what you are refusing to speak up about. Take your concerns to God

and begin to pray over your married sex life now.

7. If your MOG has overcome his problem with pornography, thank him for feeling safe enough to share and for his being honest with you. He had this problem before you, but now it's an "our" problem. Be a support to him as you try to understand his battle as it may try to creep up. Do not judge him. Do not blame yourself. It's sin! Hate it and Fight it...together! Read books on combating it, talk to your hubby when you worry and let him be himself when he needs to confess. Do whatever it takes to win and experience unencumbered intimacy.
Even if that means read <u>Every Man's Battle</u>, go to a seminar/workshop, counseling. He's worth it and obviously, he thinks you are, too to be this open, honest and including you in the pit the enemy tries to trap him in.

8. What do you think of the idea that sex is worship? When you say you're willing to do whatever God asks of you and want to please Him, remember that pleasing your husband pleases God. Will that prevent you from withholding sex from your husband when he asks? (1 Corinthians 7:3-5)

9. What can you do to protect the intimacy shared between you and your husband? What are you seeing and listening to that encourages intimacy? What is present in your environment

that invites Division and Discord? What can you do to get rid of it?

10. Have you remained steadfast in maintaining your virginity? Your renewed sexual purity? How do you feel about your decision? Has sexual pressure been difficult for you? How would you encourage others to stay the course? Has anyone mocked, ridiculed, embarrassed you by their reactions to you remaining sexually pure? What was said or done that hurt you? Did it make you second guess your decision? If so, why? What can you do to ward off doubts? What was said or done that helped you to shrug such discouragement off?

Chapter 18

It's Not About You or the Man of God

You think you want to be married so badly. Not as much as God wants you to. That is the truth, believe it or not. As the Bible says, God knew you before the foundations of the world (Ephesians 1:4). He knows the plans He has for you (Jeremiah 29:11), that includes who He has planned for you to marry. Why would God care? He cares because He loves you and He loves other people. Since, you're a Daddy's girl, a princess, you simply share the same heart, as the King for His people. What does your marriage have to do with other people? Lots!

Imagine, there are people out there in the world that only your influence will touch. The same goes for your Man of God. You both may be able to do a good work for God as individuals using your God given gifts and talents. However, it doesn't compare to the magnitude it could be once you both come together. Look at the scripture, Deuteronomy 32:30, "...one can put a thousand to flight and two can put ten thousand to flight."

Obviously, you believe you are called to be married or desire to be married; therefore, becoming one with a Man of God. Then it is God's will for you both to complete each other. Meaning, you both are missing a part of yourself that can only be found in the other. Then that means you aren't able to make the full impact for God and his kingdom, until you are made whole by coming together. God needs you both to come together for His Glory. It's a mystery as it is stated in Ephesians 5:31-32.

I believe there are people out there that are praying for Godly couples to come together. This is good, because it's not good for man to be alone or a woman since she cannot do what she was designed to do, to help her man, if she's without a man. Suppose these people that need the gospel are given a vision of who God will send to them, so God reveals this to these people in order for them to pray for these couples to come. These prayers that are offered in advance are aiding the formulation of God ordained couples into marriage. Without these married couples these people may not receive the Word of God and miss being saved.

We say that the family is the first ministry. True, the family is a ministry within itself, but it is also to do the work of the ministry. It is the smallest but the most dynamic unit in the Kingdom of God. God needs Godly marriages to produce Godly offspring to continue the spread of His gospel. Also, to reproduce spiritual children as the natural children are learning to do ministry work beside their parents.

In the beginning, my entire love affair has been solely chasing after the Lover of my soul, Jesus! I'm still very much involved in a love affair with Him as my Mighty Man of God has not entered my life as of yet. However, I don't expect that to change even once he does. The point is, before being healed of my past, my issues and my hurt, I told God that I am a warrior princess. I'm unlike the others, as I can be soft, but I am strong in Him and His Word. I want to fight in the end time harvest for souls for His kingdom. My loyalty is to Him and I will go as far as to marry whomever out of sheer obedience for strictly ministry. I don't want just any husband, the one I want is based on the biggest impact that both he and I will make for God. I wasn't interested in romance, just the adventure.

God: "I don't work that way. You can't have one without the other."

Me: "I don't want the romance that is where your heart gets involved and hurt."

I was met with only silence, meaning romance was coming. How? I don't see how it's possible. I've been too strong for too long. God did a work on me, He softened me up, it's uncomfortable as it's an unknown area for me. I still have no Man of God in my sight. Now, I'm getting antsy for both, the fight and for love. My MOG will have to teach me how to fall in love, the forever, unconditional God kind of love and hopefully I'll be able to teach him how amazing the adventure can be with us side by side.

God knows how to talk to me, as He does with you, too. To get my attention He gave me an incredible God Dream. Do you recall what a God Dream is? A God Dream, must meet the following requirements. 1) The dream must be so big it's impossible for you to do it without God. 2) You can't do the dream alone. God will bring others to fulfill the dream as a community. 3) The dream is for the benefit of others. 4) The dream outlives you and is passed onto the next generation as a legacy. God knew how seriously I would take my God Dream, therefore, He entrusted it to me.

The day came when He told me to prepare for a Mighty Man of God to enter my life. I thought having a husband, would make me weak, slow my service to God down or stop my serving altogether.

God knew my disappointment. He reassured me this wasn't the case. He told me to think of marriage as a re-assignment. God made me feel special as if He were asking a special favor of me. Causing me to wonder, who am I, Lord? "Daphne, I need you to marry this MOG. I need his God Dream to happen in order to win souls for the end time harvest. Without you, his God Dream will never happen. He needs you in his life." How could I turn down my Lord, My King, My God? He spoke to my heart, literally. He made me feel needed. He had a work that only I could do and a man for only in which I am made to love and complete. Would I work as hard to prepare for this love as I was at fighting for souls? I would have to. So, I prayed in agreement to prevent me from harboring any future resentment against my unknown Man of God. I prayed, "God I don't want to be angry at my MOG for requiring me to let my dream die once he enters my life. So, I'm asking you to make me as passionate about his God Dream, even more so than my own. This way I won't hesitate to support, encourage and push him towards it." God has done just that. I'm simply resting in Him as I wait for the MOG to enter my life so that I may join forces with him.

So, you see having the Man of God is more than simply getting married and having a family. It's about using our love, our family as a ministry and being an ultimate weapon against the enemy, the dragon, Satan. We, princesses must keep this in mind, as it is so easy to get distracted and make everything about us. Our princes love us very much, there's nothing they won't do for us. However, after awhile we missed the way it was. When

WHEN YOU'RE READY FOR THE FAIRYTALE

we enjoyed them pursuing us, fighting for us and when that ends we crave their attention, so their focus turns toward us and not on the enemy. This allows the enemy to subtly slither between us and cause us to be in division. Remember to keep all eyes on the enemy, princesses have your man's back, be ready to pray his armor on him, and wash him with the Word of God when he returns from day to day combat. He is still fighting for you, but remember he's fighting alongside of you against the enemy.

The princesses are God's secret weapon. Women are known as the heart of the home. When a warrior fights, he can be extremely trained and skilled, but if he has no heart in what he's doing, he's no good. We are called to love and care for our Men of God and to train up our children in the way of the Lord and the way that they should go according to their own gifts and talents. We have a fight on every side and for every member of our family.

I like to call us glorified dirt. The same dirt that snake, Satan slithered on is the same that is overcoming him. He may have deceived Eve, but it's time for a rematch as now it's time for God's princesses to rise up into position beside the Men of God and reclaim dominion in the end time harvest. We've prayed for laborers for the harvest, we are those laborers along with the Sons of God. Time is of the essence. The best weapon is Godly marriages. The supreme power of the universe is God's love, so we will distribute His love from within us to our husbands, children and to the world so that all may know Him.

God told me, "Daphne, when you marry your Man of God, your marriage is more than just a marriage, it's more than a ministry, it is a mission for Me from Me. There is no other man for you. You must marry the man I have for you." My response to Him was, "And there is no other man I want." When God brings you and your Man of God together and you become one flesh, in unity you form an alliance with Him. You, secret weapon princesses become God's aces in the hole. He knows He can count on His daughters. Don't settle. Do you see how imperative that you wait on God for "the one"? Embrace the man God has for you. Love him, care for him, believe in him, pray for him and fight alongside of him.

Don't allow the enemy to lie to you anymore! You do make a difference. He tries to get you worn down in the mundane tasks required of us as wives, mothers, servants of our homes and of the House of God, etc. Remember every little thing you do or say everyday counts towards the victory. That means every thought, decision, deed or conversation matters and makes a difference. No more are we to be deceived!

Homework:

1. Who is your first love? If it's not Jesus, do you see why it needs to be?

2. Did this chapter show you the bigger picture of the significance of your marriage, of your family?

3. How can you best prepare yourself to be a princess warrior for your God, your husband and your household?

4. Write down in your journal some things you think your husband may need or like to hear in order to keep going for God and to keep taking care of his family.

5. Did this chapter help you see how the enemy tries to come against our marriages and families by distraction in communication, thought attacks, etc.?

6. Do you recognize your importance in your role in the Kingdom of God as a wife, mother and daughter of God?

DAPHNE M. HUNTER

Chapter 19

Taking Marriage Seriously

What is marriage? In my own understanding, I wouldn't know how to answer this question. As I asked God to give me a definition, this truly beautiful thought came to mind. Marriage is the coming together of a man and a woman in all selflessness to offer the best gift they have to benefit the other for a lifetime.

People may have their own expectations for the roles of a husband and a wife, so be sure to discuss your expectations in pre-marital counseling to avoid any surprises. Remember only the roles establish by God will work in such a union. Before describing what those roles are, I would like to address some areas that are seriously lacking in today's culture and even in some marriages. These areas are not husband or wife specific; therefore, they should be regarded by both and in order to be prevented.

It's sad to say that nowadays people are simply missing common courtesy. If our culture is deficient of it, then how do we expect to see it modeled in today's marriages? For example, my heart is grieved as I hear how spouses speak to each other, with harsh tones, curse words and mumbling under their breath. I cringe when I hear wives belittle their husbands or when husbands neglect their wives for other things that they consider more important. I don't expect to be the perfect wife or have the model marriage, as the Man of God and myself are still human, but I do plan on following the Word of God in my marriage as best as I can. The Bible says, "By this shall all men know that you are my disciples, if you have love for one another." (John 13:35, Eph. 5:22-25) I look to the world as what not to do and it causes me to cling to my Jesus and His Word all the more and to seek what to do. I know the best way to please my Lord is to reverence Him first and then my husband. The only way I can do this is out of obedience because I love my Jesus, My God so much, I don't know any different than what He tells me and shows me.

If ever in question about how to live out our marriages in the Godly way, read Ephesians 5:21-33. So often we hear or are even taught, wives submit to your husbands and we are to do that. However, it seems that verse 21 is often forgotten and is so vital. Marriage is about the husband and the wife submitting to one another as they would submit unto the Lord. Whereas verse 22, is too familiar and often used improperly about the wifely submission to a husband. Go back to verse 21, it states that a husband is to submit respectfully to his counterpart as she does the same to her covering. Somehow that verse ministers and touches me deeply. How strong and yet gentle a husband's leadership can be illustrated in that verse alone.

We, princesses need to understand the roles of a husband, so we know what qualities to add to our list, so we know how to pray and know what to expect to prevent settling for anything less. The Godly husband we want should be willing to do the following:

1) Be the Spiritual Leader

2) Love their wife

3) Aim to make their wife happy and fulfilled

4) To provide and protect their wife

5) To nourish and cherish their wife as someone very valuable

6) Leave the past and/or parents' habits behind

7) Become one in thought, deed and communication

8) Enjoy being united, close and affectionate

Now for our part to be the wives God has called us to be. These 4 principles given to us should be kept before us if we want to truly appreciate the gift of a husband.

1) In submitting to your husband doesn't mean to be a doormat and cannot express your mind. It means to be adaptable to his leadership, with a good attitude as we wives, go in the direction the husband leads.

2) With the husband as the head of the home, wives are to cover your husband in love, faith and prayer, while helping and encouraging him to enter his destiny.

3) Respect, enjoy and play with your husband.

4) Create a loving and peaceful refuge for our husbands in our arms and within the home

In order to stay inspired as a wife remember...

1) If you and your husband are extreme opposites, don't be discouraged, opposites do attract and usually turns out to be quite a complementary couple. Embrace each other's differences; you are learning first-hand how to see things differently.

2) Your husband can't exist or succeed without you because you complete him. He needs your help, encouragement and prayers.

3) Your marriage will be dysfunctional until you accept your role as the wife. You are not the leader or in control, because God didn't grant you that position. God establishes order and He designed how the home should be maintained.

4) Crucify your flesh and your will the moment these thoughts enter your mind. What about me? I can do a better job than my husband. (These thoughts are selfish and reflects the Jezebel Spirit of usurping authority and trying to take control.)

5) Don't try to change your husband, accept and love him.

6) Appreciate and admire him sincerely, wholeheartedly and let him know that you do regularly.

7) If you don't know if you are helping, encouraging or supporting your husband the

way you should, simply ask him. Otherwise, you're not doing your job if he doesn't feel strengthened, encouraged or supported.

8) Ask your husband, "What can I do to help you?" How can I pray for you? Look for the things you can do for him, especially those things that you don't want to do. (That's why it's called sacrifice.)

9) Should your husband become passive in any area, ask him what's wrong rather than jumping at the chance to take control or complain or belittle him.

10) Find out what your husband likes and do those things often. Whatever he doesn't like, avoid those things. Learn and discover or even try new things together to be creative and avoid boredom.

11) The wife decides if her husband is truly loving her like Christ loves the Church. If you're feeling unloved, let your husband know instead of thinking he can read your mind. This will prevent resentment, bitterness and unforgiveness.

12) Make an agreement never to say the "D" word (divorce), it's not included in your vocabulary. Find out what generational curses you and the MOG have and break them! Be willing to pray and fast together!

13) Live to create memories for and with your husband and family.

Something that I take extremely seriously is the term covenant. Marriage is a form of covenant. So, I cannot be at peace with myself without discussing the significance of the Marriage Covenant. What is covenant? Covenant means to "cut" and is a binding agreement between two parties that cannot be broken not even by death. Therefore, explaining why the line is said in the marriage vows stating, "...until death do us part."

In the Bible, a Blood Covenant was established between God, the Father and God, the Son, Jesus and is the reason why Jesus' sacrificial death satisfies the payment of our sin. There are 9 steps that must be fulfilled in order to enter into covenant. It's these same 9 steps that are present in the Marriage Covenant. It's important to me for you to know these steps. I believe it will help you in taking your future marriage seriously.

Why is sharing this with you so important to me? Well, because for a while I would plan and coordinate weddings as a hobby. Once I realized the traditions performed in the wedding ceremony and at the reception modeled the covenant steps, I not only appreciated the wedding, but the marriage in a whole new way. I want you to see this for yourself. Then your wedding and reception will no longer be a ritual or tradition of men, but of a Holy consequence between you and your husband-to-be with your Maker.

Covenant Steps vs. Wedding Traditions

Step 1. Take off Coat or Robe – symbolically means, "I'm giving you all of myself. I am pledging my life to you.

This is represented by 1) the bride walking down the aisle by forsaking all others to become one with the groom waiting for her 2) when they speak their marriage vows with heartfelt sincerity 3) the lifting of her veil and 4) them both disrobing on their honeymoon.

Step 2. Take off Belt – symbolically means, "I'm giving all of my strength, support and protection to you."

This is represented in the wedding once the father "gives away" his daughter to the groom charging her new husband to take care of her by offering her his support, protection and provision.

Step 3. Cut the Covenant – symbolically means the commitment they both are entering into, by saying, "I'm dying to myself and giving up the rights to my own life and beginning a new life with you as my covenant partner until death."

Once the Man of God proposes, he is basically saying, "I'm giving up the right to remain single and asking you to join me in covenant. This is accomplished by them both once the vows are carried out on the wedding day.

Step 4. Raise the Right Arm and Mix Blood – Upon entering into covenant the two parties would cut their right palms and intermingle their blood; therefore, becoming "blood brothers" as a symbol of their agreement.

In the marriage bed, once the marriage is consummated, the husband would penetrate his virgin bride and she would bleed slightly from her hymen being broken during sex. Therefore, blood would confirm her virginity, which would seal the covenant. The Blood of Jesus confirms in agreement the uniting of the Bride & Groom that are committed to Him.

Step 5. Exchange Names – Each covenant partner would take on the last name of the other as part of their new name.

Obviously, this is when the bride takes on the surname of her husband.

(Note: It is completely up to your discretion of how you choose to handle your new last name. Below I share a valid argument.)

I discussed with God my feelings about how I felt about the exchange of names. I felt that in dropping my surname I would lose my identity or all the work I had accomplished to make my own family (name) proud would now be credited to my husband. Names are significant and very important to me. So, I wanted to consider hyphenating my last name in the future. One argument is that all my old past associated with my name would be dragged into my new future with my husband. I would be tarnishing my new start, my new life. Why would I want to bring something old, dead and gone into a new, alive and promising future and then put that onto my husband as we would become one? Then questioned was my not wanting to let go of my own last name be nothing more than pride? If so, then I would have to die to myself. I know I would be proud to carry my husband's surname.

Giving it more thought makes me more proud of whoever he is and whatever my new last name would be. Why? Because I won't accept a MOG that doesn't live up to his name and having his surname would make me brand new, with a new beginning. Plus, all a husband has to offer that is truly his to his wife is his name. The same name that covers her as it is the name to be written in the Lamb's Book of Life.

Another reasonable argument in favor of keeping my maiden name was, I have recently suffered the death of my father and wanting to hold onto my last name to honor him has resurfaced. Therefore, again questioning, "What my last name will be?" My father was the only male and with me being his only child, the family name will die off with him should I take on my husband's last name. Instead of deciding now, I think this will be a subject to discuss with my MOG. I want to be as respectful to my husband as much as I want to be to my father and his memory. As you can see the decision regarding the wife's last name is a very personal decision and should be carefully considered by both, you and your MOG.

Step 6. Make a Scar – Visible proof that these two parties were in covenant and to ward off any intruders.

The exchange of wedding rings is visible proof that you both are in a committed marriage relationship and is to ward off undesirable attention from outsiders.

Step 7. Give Covenant Terms – Before witnesses you would state that all your assets (money, property and possessions) and liabilities would become each other's. Should one covenant partner die, the other would take on their family.

This is expressed in the marriage vows when spoken, "...for richer or for poorer..." before the congregation at the wedding ceremony. Also, when you sign the marriage license you are legally taking on the financial responsibility of one another and establishing a larger, stronger family with both respective families.

Step 8. Eat a Memorial Meal – would complete the covenant union. Bread and wine would be served. The bread would be broken into 2 pieces and fed to each other saying, "This is symbolic of my body and I'm now putting it into you." Then they would serve each other the wine and say, "This is symbolic of my life blood which is now your blood; therefore, I'm in you and you're in me."

In some wedding ceremonies a couple may choose to have communion to honor this covenant step as well as focus their oneness with their relationship with God. Otherwise, this may be represented at the reception, once the bride and groom serves and feeds each other cake or drink from wine glasses as they intertwine their arms for a sip.

Step 9. Plant a Memorial – By planting a tree, this explains the Cross of Jesus.

In order to remember this special occasion, party favors are given to the guests with the bride and groom's names and/or wedding date on them.

Some have given flower seeds as a way of keeping with planting an actual memorial.

I hope this gives you a different mindset as you plan your wedding and you reflect with creativity what all the steps mean to make your Big Day more personalized.

Homework:

1. Do you have other inspirational suggestions to add to the list for wives or husbands to take marriage seriously? Any suggestions for personalizing a wedding?

2. If anything, what did you learn about marriage or covenant that you didn't know or consider before?

3. Which verse regarding the marriage roles means the most to you and why? List one verse for the husband and one for the wife.

DAPHNE M. HUNTER

Chapter 20

Doing Life Together

This will probably be my hardest chapter to write, since I am not currently living this one out myself. All I know is, as couples we cannot look to each other to make the other happy. That is each person's own responsibility. So, if you're feeling empty inside, don't expect your husband to fill you, go to God for a refill. Before you have a husband, you and God have survived some obstacles and situations that you might have thought you needed a man to aid you to overcome. Therefore, you must continue to rely on your own personal relationship with God to fight your own personal individual battles. It is not your husband's responsibility as Spiritual Leader to take on your spiritual burdens. Otherwise, you place unfair pressure on him and set both of you up for failure. Remember to do life together, not do life for them. Also, don't forget that you are not to become your husband's life. You simply want to do life together. What is doing life together mean? It means to create memories and enjoy life's experiences together. To have someone to come home to and share all that happened during the day, or to spend time with them or show them something you discovered and enjoy their reaction.

Life isn't easy, so doing life isn't either. Like anything, marriage requires work and don't expect the work to be equally shared 50/50. As you both grow and expectations change, communicate that and renegotiate to prevent bitterness, hostility and resentment. The best thing to do is to stay open to each other's way of talking, sharing, listen, recognize and learn each other's moods, ask when in doubt, write notes, don't assume anything and don't generalize.

To keep the fun in marriage, find a shared activity you already both like to do, or pick one you both have never done before so you can learn it together. Continue to have date-nights. Find out what the definition of being romantic means to each other and then try to out-do the other when feeling like being romantic. What haven't you done before and do it for the first time together and keep a list of all your "firsts". Reminisce often, remind each other what it was that caught your eye, what you love about them the most, what personality quirk you think is adorable, etc. Never stop learning about each other, continue to study about improving your relationship, communication, have Bible study as a couple, family, etc.

You may be ready for your fairytale romance; however, the only happily ever after ending we have here on earth, is the daily success of each day's victory until we go to Heaven. So, in the meantime, learn, love and serve Jesus! Respect, love and appreciate your husband! Nurture, love and take care of yourself, your family and your home! And don't forget to live life loudly and enjoy the greatest adventure that God has given you...to love Him, Life and each other!

Homework:

1. What advice would you give to keep the peace at home, to share the work in order to keep a positive environment?

2. What other suggestions do you have to keep the romance alive in your future marriage?

3. Why do you think wives would want to dump their responsibility to fight their own spiritual battles onto their husbands? Did you feel like you were only holding down the fort until the MOG arrived? If so, why? Do you see how unfair this is to the MOG?

4. How do you prevent the temptation from unfairly dumping on your husband?

   I admit I believed a lie. The lie told me that because I am a woman that makes me a weaker vessel meaning my spiritual attacks are to be proportionate to what a woman can handle. When the attacks were overwhelming, they felt man-sized I thought how unfair for me to be dealt such circumstances not having a man to aid me to conquer them. I went to God about this only to be chastened, that there is no such thing. His truth was found in the verse of Galatians 3:28. Men and women are seen as equals before God and Satan. Therefore, I had no excuse to not be able to fight on my own. I must admit each time I was victorious I surprised myself that I had what it takes to beat the enemy without depending on a man.

5. Read and meditate on Matthew 25:1-13 to be a wise virgin.

This chapter concludes Book 1 – "Getting Ready" in the series of "When You're Ready For The Fairytale: What To Do While Waiting For The Prince". I invite you to continue on this journey of your heart being healed, whether you're single desiring to be married or if you're married and desiring to be a better wife, in order to have a better marriage or simply you want to be the Bride that Christ desires you to be.

It would be my honor and privilege if you allow me to continue to join you by having you begin Book 2 – "Still Waiting" in the series.

The Ultimate Revelation

Remember the point isn't about wanting or needing to be married. Getting married is about offering the greatest sacrifice, to commit your lifetime and be willing to die for another which is the ultimate price and places you in a position to become more holy. God says, "Be Holy as I am Holy." (Leviticus 20:7) Then remember being married is being Christ-like, that there's no greater love than when a brother (sister) lays down their life for another. (John 15:13) To love one another as you love yourself, is being obedient to His commandments. If we love Him, we will keep His commandments. (Matthew 22: 37-40) So He tells us, "Husbands love your wives as Christ loved the church that He gave Himself up for her and wives submit yourselves to your own husbands as you submit until the Lord. (Ephesians 5:21, 25 - suggested reading Eph. 5:19-31)

The preparation experienced wasn't achieved to solely be ready to marry the Man of God, but to be ready to experience miracles in every area of your life. The purpose was to learn, grow, mature and be prepared to live the God kind of life, a Zoe Life, to live life more abundantly (John 10:10) by living the God-Dream, your Fairytale here on earth until Christ's return.

Be Free to Love, to Give, to Do and to Be.

Keep Dreaming. Believe in the Dream. Live the Dream.

Do whatever it takes and obtain the God-Dream!

YOU ARE READY!!!

Now GO!!!

DAPHNE M. HUNTER

The Happy Ending

I had no idea what I was to write for a Happy Ending. All of our happy endings are entrusted to the Author of our Love Stories. The True Happy Ending I look forward to is being united with Him in Heaven, our Final Home. However, until then allow these words that managed to find themselves on a page addressed to you bless you.

You, princess, truly deserve a very real-life happy ending of your very own. I am so very proud of you and that you have journeyed through this book from beginning to end. I hope, pray and trust that you have grown considerably. Thank you for allowing me to play a minor role in your fairytale.

I was simply the vessel and He, the Holy Spirit did the writing. Remember the Holy Spirit can only reveal what the Father says and does. Therefore, these chapters were guideposts of what I experienced while led by the Holy Spirit on my journey being single. I pray you recognized such guideposts along your own journey and that you didn't feel so alone, because you're not. Keep believing and know it is truly Him that is the Author and the Finisher of our faith, of our journey and of these words in this book.

Please Remember…

Every day is an opportunity to make a new happy ending.

I, your sister, Daphne M. Hunter do believe in you, the Jesus in you, the call on your life and stand in full agreement with the plans the Lord has in store for you, not only for your Man of God, but the fruit of this journey, the family, the ministry and the God-Dream acquired from your faith walk. Remember none of these were easy to obtain, but all will be and were well worth it!

Your future is worth fighting for and so are the souls you'll win!

It's War, Soldier – Warrior Princess! Take up your armor of God, stay strong, stay focused, fight hard and claim your victory!

In the King's Service - a fellow Warrior Princess,

Daughter of the Most High God and your sister-in-Christ,

Rev. Daphne M. Hunter

With much hope, faith and love I write this in the Spirit of the Lord with His love and encouragement for you. This closing prayer to you is my final gift from your Father God, the King.

My Dearest Daughter,

"Baby Girl, I love you! I know you. I know what you're called to be.

I fashioned you myself. So, trust me! I know the road. I know where you're going. I know how you're going to get there. I know it all.

I am your all in all. Trust Me!"

You don't know how, so let it go! Don't try to figure it out. I'll bring it to you, just stay open. This is powerful! Even when others criticize, mock or tell you differently don't let their words harden your heart. Stay willing to serve me and the people I call you to serve. Above all keep an open heart and mind. You know why you need to keep an open heart, but why an open mind? To you in the natural, what I may ask you to do may seem "crazy", a completely illogical thing to do, but then you'll know it's definitely me!

I know you love me, due to your obedience thus far; however, I want more. More of you, I want you and I to experience a whole new level of intimacy. Let's birth a "New Thing". Be ready! Be excited! You're moving up with me! I love you so much I can't let you stay where you are and how you've been. I want you closer to me. Why do you think I am preparing a place for you? Until then, I'll come back for you like I promised from time to time to keep you focused and on track, as you make time to be with me.

So, please stay in communication with me, my beloved.

Love the Lover of your Soul,

Jesus

DAPHNE M. HUNTER

Do You Want to Become a Princess?

You've come to the right place if you do and are…

Needing a Personal Relationship with God, the King and want to become His Royal Daughter, His Princess…

We all know in order to be a princess your daddy must be a king. Well, there is a King that wants you to be His daughter, a princess in His Kingdom. He wants to bless you with spiritual blessings and give you eternal gifts and even your very own fairytale romance. Before sending you an earthly prince He wants to love on you and…be your first love!

There was a Prince that came for you and sacrificed His life and died for you and His name is Jesus Christ. He wants to be your personal Lord and Savior. He wants to forgive you of all your mess, all your mistakes and all your sin from the past, present and future with His blood. He will offer you a new clean slate, a new life and a new way of doing things. With your permission, you will be accepted and adopted into His royal family and become a princess. IF you are serious about making a life change and a commitment to Jesus, then please say these words aloud as you confess Jesus as Lord.

Dear Jesus,

I come to you right now and offer you all of my heart and the rest of my life because I want a serious 100% committed relationship with you. I believe you died on the cross and rose again just for me. Please forgive me of all my sins and make me brand new. Make me into the princess I have only dreamt of being. Thank you for my fresh start and my new life with you. There is no one I would rather spend eternity with than you. You have patiently loved and waited for me knowing this time would come. Fill me now with your Holy Spirit so that I may hear you clearly as I commit to learn, follow and serve you. I am willing to learn how to love you, trust in you as well as entrust my fairytale romance to be written by you. Thank you for loving, accepting and embracing me by becoming my personal Lord and Savior.

In your Mighty & Precious Name, Jesus, I pray.

Amen!

Sweet Princess,

Here what to do next, now that you are a Christian and a Princess!

1. Welcome to the Family of God! Congratulations for making the very best decision of your life!

2. Please fill out the enclosed RSVP card to the King's Wedding invitation to celebrate with Him in Heaven at the Wedding Feast! This card states that you just accepted Jesus into your heart and life and have become a Princess today! Be sure you mail it!

2. Next, you need to get a Bible, any translation is fine. However, these translations are easier to understand.

   New International Version (NIV)
   New King James Version (NKJV)
   New Living Translation (NLT)
   The Amplified Bible (AMP)
   The Message (MSG)

4. Find a church that focuses on the Bible and on your relationship with

God, not a religion about God. The right church for you will be full of other princesses as you learn the culture and the language of the kingdom that you reign in.

Dear Princess:

I want to sincerely thank you for allowing me to travel with you on this personal journey and for being a small part of your very own Fairytale!

If this book really touched your heart and ministered to you, please feel free to contact me and share what spoke to you the most. I especially want to hear from you if you became a Princess simply from reading this book as well as interested in your very own love story. You are welcome to send a letter, email or use social media to contact me! Got a photo of you and your prince even better! I know your fairytale will inspire me as I await mine.

God Bless You and Keep You!

Don't Forget! If you have become a New Princess to the Kingdom let me know, so that I may be encouraged by all the new princesses joining the family!

Sign another

Daughter of the Most High God,

Princess Daphne M. Hunter

About the Author

Reverend Daphne M. Hunter lives in southern California and is a mother of 3 adult children. She has a daughter, Kiana (whose name means Princess), and two sons, Jordan and Benjamin. Her home church is The Rock Church & World Outreach Center in San Bernardino, where Daphne is the Deaf Ministry Leader for the last 17 years.

Daphne has a BIG heart for serving others. Her heart's desire is to minister to the "spiritually deaf" (meaning anyone who doesn't know Jesus), women, singles, marrieds and the Deaf Community. Daphne doesn't want to limit God or how He chooses to use her for His Glory. However, so far she has been used predominantly for the deaf, singles and most recently for the women and youth ministries.

She has graduated from The Rock School of Ministry (now known as The Rock Bible College) in 2005, and from Good Shepherd Ministries - International School of Ministry in 2007. She is deeply honored to be the ASL Interpreter for the ISOM-ASL Bible College Curriculum for the Deaf, she now is an in classroom facilitator for future deaf leaders to graduate from the same program. Since 2003, Daphne has served at LifeHouse Theater in various roles, but is most known for interpreting their performances. Therefore, interpreting for The Rock Church and World Outreach Center, Good Shepherd Ministries' ISOM-ASL and for LifeHouse Theater and Productions, Inc. was the beginning of her preparation to be launched into local and international ministry.

She seeks to use her signing ability to aid in the educating and increasing awareness of the deaf to the Body of Christ regarding its need to reach the Deaf people, to ensure that the gospel reaches the Deaf worldwide. God has granted this desire as of August 1, 2016, Rev. Daphne will host D.E.A.F. To The World TV program on Holy Spirit Broadcasting Network (HSBN.TV)

As for the women, she prays to see women freed from their bondages and emerge as the princesses they already are and cheer them on as they embark on their journeys with their God given talents. Another of her biggest joys is to encourage others to finding their God-Dreams and to promote the Arts through Drama, Music, Dance, Painting, Sculpture, Filmmaking, Poetry and Creative Writing, etc. to redeem the arts of any medium for God's Glory.

In addition to signing, writing, speaking and sharing her testimony, Daphne enjoys talking and listening to the hearts of others, teaching the Word of God, reading, listening to music, signing to music, plays board & card games, air hockey, tennis, bowling, gardening and loves to watch movies. Last but not least, she enjoys journaling to her Mighty Man of God as she waits for her Godly Romance to play out just like all of you.

Ministry Contact Information

Rev. Daphne M. Hunter
P.O. Box 11535
San Bernardino, CA 92423

PrincessFellowship@gmail.com

www.ingramcontent.com/pod-product-compliance
Lightning Source LLC
Chambersburg PA
CBHW071421090426
42737CB00011B/1529